For more information, visit www.jrrothstein.com.

First Hardcover Edition, September 2020.

Library of Congress Control Number: 2020917774

ISBN#: 978-1-7353986-1-7

וזכני לגדל
בנים ובני בנים
חכמים ונבונים
׳אוהבי ה
יראי אלקים
אנשי אמת
זרע קדש
בה׳ דבקים
ומאירים את העולם
בתורה ובמעשים טובים
ובכל מלאכת
עבודת הבורא

May I merit to raise children and grandchildren,
those who are wise,
intelligent and understanding,
who love and fear God,
and who always speak the truth.

May my descendants be a holy legacy,
who cleave to the divine.
May they be lights to the world,
lights filled with Torah and good deeds,
and be of service to the creator and his creations.

- The prayer of Esther Sarah Dubrow and
Rabbi Zvi Hirsch Poretzky

Introduction

Through the lens of two Jewish families, this books attempts to capture the lives of the inhabitants of Tolochin, Belarus, a classical *shtetl*, prior to its destruction during the Holocaust.

The book traces the family history of two Jewish families, the Poretzkys and the Rutsteins, the events surrounding their persecution in the pogroms of the dawn of the twentieth century, their resettlement as refugees in the United States, as well as the rise to fame of their most famous son, Jacob Rutstein.

It is through this book, modeled after the *yizkor* books of yore, that I hope their memories will be memorialized and their legacies endure.

Yehuda Rothstein
New York, New York
October 1, 2020

TABLE OF CONTENTS

PART I

HISTORICAL OVERVIEW OF JEWISH TOLOCHIN, BELARUS

Before the Russian Revolution, the Jews of White Russia, a region which covers most of modern-day Belarus, including the shtetl or village of Tolochin, were forced to live in a region known as the "Pale of Settlement," which spanned from the Baltic Sea to the Black Sea. About five million Jews (94% of the total Jewish population, about 12% of the Russian population) lived in this region. The poverty rate was high. The Jews had the worst jobs and worked for the lowest wages and in the most demeaning positions. Pogroms occurred frequently throughout the Russian Empire. Tolochin or Talachyn (Belarusian: Талачын, Łacinka: Tałačun, pronounced [taɫaˈtʂɨn]) or Tolochin (Russian: Толо́чин; Polish: Tołoczyn,

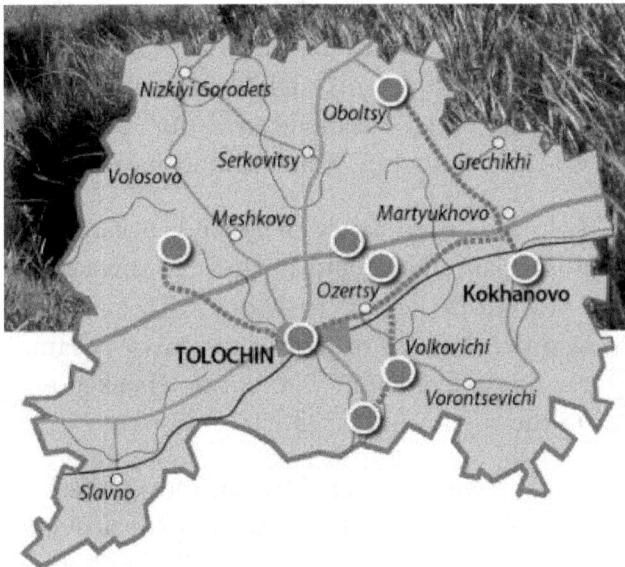

Map of the region around Tolochin

Lithuanian: Talačynas, and Yiddish: טאָלאָטשין) was and is a small village in the Viciebsk Region of Belarus, an administrative center of the Talachyn district. It is perhaps the coldest city in Belarus in winter, with a record low of -42.2C. The hamlet of Tolochin was founded in 1433 in the Vitebsk province of the Grand Duchy of Lithuania (which later became the Kingdom of Lithuania.) The town ran across a famous trade route, and for this reason, the city was often subjected to conquest, destruction, and ruin through the centuries.

In 1604, Lev Ivanovich Sapieha founded here a Christian Basilian monastery, a hospital, and a school. Since at least the mid-17th century, Tolochin became a significant center of trade, and the settlement held major market fairs at least three times a year. During the war between Russia and the Polish-Lithuanian Commonwealth (1654-1667), the hamlet had 314 houses which were all burned down.

Some claim that the town itself was first settled by Jews. Other references suggest a Jewish presence as early as the 16th century, while others place it as only beginning as late as 1717. However, from the third quarter of the 17th century, historical documents mention Jewish settlements in the greater Tolochin region – settlements such as Bobr, Belynichi, Gory, Glusk, Dubrovno, Krynki, Mir, Ross, Staroselie, and our Tolochin. In 1766, 648 Jews were enrolled in the Tolochin Kahal and its parishes.

In 1772, Tolochin, then a city of Poland, became a border crossing point between the Russian empire and Poland. In this city, as an important settlement on the way from Poland to Moscow, a custom house was also established. At this time, the eastern part of the town became Old Tolochin and the Western part New Tolochin. The border check-point and a customs house functioned in the town until 1793.

John Ledyard, the American explorer and adventurer, visited Tolochin in or around 1788. After several weeks of traveling, he arrived at the Russian-Polish borderlands. The region was a thicket of disputed boundaries between numerous states, with Tolochin at its center. Ledyard describes his journey to the Drut River, from which he crossed into Poland, and entered Tolochin.

3

He writes:

At last, the dear moment came that I was conducted over a Bridge across a little River, across the Barrier into the little Village Tolochin in Poland.... I was conducted for quarters to the house of a Jew. Not being permitted to enter the Dominions of a people more destitute of principle than themselves, they hover about its boundaries here in great numbers. It was a large dirty house filled with dirt & noise & children.... [The region] is besides almost solely inhabited by Jews who are ever nuisances except in places totally Commercial.

The Jews of Tolochin were at the center of the Russian Empire's decision to censor Jewish books. In or around 1790, Jewish books were imported by Tolochin locals from Poland into the town. The Governor of the Tolochin region, General Passek, discovered these books as they passed through Tolochin. Upon their inspection at the custom house, the authorities ordered the Jewish books to be detained and confiscated. Catherine II of Russia, upon learning that Jewish books were being imported into the Russian Empire, thereupon took the informal local ban and formally prohibited the importation of Hebrew books throughout the Russian Empire. The edict provided that the Jews could obtain their supplies of religious literature only from Russian printers.

Around the same time, the famous Rabbi Shlomo of Tolochin, who was one of the greatest disciples of the Vilna Goan, Rabbi Eliyahu Kraner of Vilna (known as the Vilner Gaon or Gra), migrated to the holy land. Rabbi Shlomo was the only one among the Gaon's disciples to make *aliya* emigrate to the Land of Israel while his teacher was still alive. Rabbi Shlomo of Tolochin reached the Land of Israel on the first of the month of Nissan, 1794. He was known as a great Torah scholar and a miracle worker. Research creates the impression that Tolochin had a minimal *Chasidic* presence and that its inhabitants considered themselves "Litvaks" under the guidance of the Vilna Goan and his disciples.

The horrid living conditions of those living within Jewish Tolochin continued to astound those outsiders that visited, like John Ledyard. Napoleon Bonaparte and his expedition on November 22, 1812 passed through Tolochin during his eastern military expedition and encountered local Jews living in poverty. The terrible crowding of the Jewish population of Tolochin was the result of formal government measures to evict Jews from the countryside to cities and towns. History records numerous complaints and petitions to the state from the Jews of the region. For example, in 1825, the Jews of Tolochin characterized their situation as follows: "from great oppression in one house of two or more families, they were punished by extreme poverty so that we can't have any daily food."

New Tolochin or "Zarechny Tolochin" was founded in the second quarter of the 19th century on the western bank of the Drut River and was a part of the Mogilev province of the Russian Empire which had previously incorporated the town. The word "old" or "Starro" was added in due course to the name of the original part of the town. In the 1870s, the Tolochin railroad station (Moscow–Brest) was built four (4) kilometers outside of town. In 1880, Old Tolochin had 160 wooden houses, 110 of which belonged to Jewish families. New Tolochin had 93 houses, 27 of which were Jewish. There were also four houses made of stone – three in Old Tolochin and one in the new part. On the whole, 1,119 Jews were working in Old Tolochin and 253 in New Tolochin in 1880. In 1886, Old Tolochin had three Jewish schools and numerous synagogues.

In 1888, a boy was born in the family of Moysi and Lei Baileen. The newborn was called Israel Baileen. In 1893, the family moved to New York. Israel in America became the famous Irving Berlin. In 1911, Irving created the famous Alexander's Ragtime Band. He would become one of Tolochin's most famous children.

Between 1750 to 1940, the Jews of Tolochin constituted the overwhelming majority of the population, at times as high as 90%. This created a great sense of attachment by the local Jews to the village, which can be categorized as a classical shtetl. Shprintsy (Sophia) Lvovna Rohkind (1903–

5

2000), a well-known linguistic scholar, author of a Yiddish-Russian dictionary, and a native of Tolochin, in her unpublished memoirs, described the pride the local Jews felt towards their town. She writes:

> *Tolochin is my homeland and the homeland of our ancestors - preserved in my soul as a memory of childhood and adolescence, about close and dear people, about family joys and sorrows, about what is dear to every person, which cannot be forgotten even until old age.*

According to a former Jewish resident of Tolochin, Anatoloy Schneider, the Russian authorities put a lot of effort into the military and financial development of this region. People from other towns would come to Tolochin to buy things – there were a lot of wholesale shops, stores, kiosks, and a big trade square. Jews were traditionally involved in selling timber, cereals, vodka, fish, confectionery, and small wares. Jews were also known to be excellent craftsmen: blacksmiths, potters, tailors, shoemakers, tanners, barbers, and bakers. Trade, however, remained their major occupation and the Jewish inhabitants were heavily dependent on the trade fairs, and other trade-related migration. The shops sold groceries, haberdashery, pottery, fabrics, clothes, and meat. Fish was brought three times a week from places that had lakes or rivers.

Schneider also describes the geographic layout of Tolochin. The shops were also close to the post office and the telegraph. Craftsmen also lived here: tailors, shoemakers, and blacksmiths. The street ended with a highway. Immediately after the market square, the main street - Orsha Street (now Lenin Street) began. On it were a large synagogue and two smaller ones. Men prayed on the first floor of the large synagogue, women prayed on the second floor. At the synagogue courtyard, wedding ceremonies usually took place. The crowds brought the groom and the bride, accompanied by relatives and friends, put up a chuppah (wedding canopy) and held the wedding ceremony.

Zarechnaya (Zarechenskaya) Street, now Engels Street, was one of the longest. It began near the bazaar, crossed the Drut River, and stretched far to the west, intersected by many alleys and streets. The street lighting was bad. In some places, the kerosene lamps were dimly lit. The main source of lighting was a weak light falling from the windows of the houses. Not all the streets in Tolochin were paved. In the fall, they had to walk on the dirt; only on the sides were wooden sidewalks. The streets were poorly lit. Here and there, lanterns with kerosene lamps were near the houses, but mostly they were satisfied with the light from the windows, which were also not very abundant.

A big challenge for the city was frequent fires. The housing stock consisted mainly of wooden buildings and fires occurred frequently. In 1897, a Jewish fire brigade was created in the city. As evidenced by the archival documents, the members of the squad had good training and discipline. A newspaper report captures one such fire which occurred in 1884:

> The fire which took place on the 10th of March destroyed the Jewish community mikva and five private houses with their belongings. The owners of the houses were local Jews: Israel Berka Rodshtein, Leiba Zusin, Chaya-Ryvka Khotovkin, Abram, and David Alkins.
>
> The investigation showed that on the night of March 9, a local peasant, Ivan Shopik, was using the stove to make the mikva warm and negligently fell asleep. The fire began and destroyed all the neighboring houses belonging to the named above persons.
>
> The fire has damaged Staro-Tolochin Jewish community for 2000 rubles, Rodshtein for 1000 rubles, Zusin for 300 rubles, Khotovkin for 150 rubles, Abram Alkin for 650 rubles, Dovid Alkin for 50 rubles, and Ryzh for 100 rubles.[1]

However, not all fires in Tolochin were accidents. Many were arson attacks by non-Jews against their Jewish neighbors in the contexts of pogroms.

---

[1] Mogilevskie Gubernskie Vedomosti, 1884, #32

Pogroms against the Jewish community occurred frequently throughout the 1890s and the first decade of the twentieth century.

Irving Berlin, the great American composer and musician, and Tolochin's most famous son, told his first biographer, Alexander Woollcott, that his first memory occurred laying with the rest of his family beside a dirt road, wrapped in a blanket at night, watching as his home and other homes in Jewish Tolochin being burned in a pogrom by non-Jews. Aaron (Harry) Paretzky, a Tolochin resident, reported that in approximately 1900, non-Jewish locals rounded up some of Tolochin's Jews, herded them into one of the local synagogue's, and lit the building on fire. These Jews consisted of women, old men, and children. They were freed by Aaron, along with a group of teenage boys who had been hunting and/or playing in the forest. The group, upon returning to the village, heard the cries of their friends and family in the process of being burned alive. The boys broke up the door of the synagogue which had been bolted shut and freed their co-villagers.

The poverty, the violence against Jews, and a wave of new ideas radicalized some segments of the local Jewish population of Tolochin. The following is an account of some of the social unrest in Tolochin and should be viewed as a local variant of the type of national unrest that would continue for years, and eventually culminate in the Russian Revolution of 1917. The account, found in an official history of the revolution, is as follows[2]:

Apart from the said above, as my duty requires me to do, I am reporting to Your Excellency that in the parish of Orsha, a local police chief went to investigate the situation in Tolochin with a platoon of dragoons for reasons of civilian riots – similar to the ones that happened in Kopis, Lyadi, and Shklovo. As the police

---

[2] The selection is a translation of an excerpt from the following book: Дъло 1905 год у Беларусі. Зборнік архіуных дакументау. Менск 1925. Цэнтральная комісія ЦВК БССР па азначэньню 20-х гадовага юбілею рэволюцыі 1905 году і гістпарт цэнтральнага комітэту кп(б)Б Зборнік архіуных дакумэнтау пад рэдакцыяй С. Агурскага, Б. Аршанскага і Іл. Барашки Дзяржаунае выдавецтва Беларусі Менск-1926, page 219.

chief's investigation reported, the people participating in the riots were solely local youth up to 200 people.

The following [Jewish] individuals stood out of the crowd as leaders and guiding hands: Shepshel Izrin (Шепшель Изрин), Haim Diment (Хаим Дымент), Josel Rutstein (Йосель Рутштейн), Sholom Rozh (Шолом Рож), Zalman Korlin (Залман Корлин), Jankel Levin (Янкель Левин), who shouted: "make away with the tsar, monarchy, priesthood, government, capitalism, police; long live a republic of freedom." They held, taking turns, a red flag with a title. It is not yet known what the title said. The only thing that was clearly seen was a big letter "D".

Some people were walking in front of the crowd, armed with revolvers and shot more than anybody else. As the police chief reported, in Tolochin they escaped or hid with his permission, with peace persisting while he was there.

Today I received a telegram from the police chief reporting that once the dragoons that he needed to visit prince Lyoubomirsky's mansion left, the youth of Tolochin began to do daring violence to the local population. Taking into account that the police chief needs the half-squadron of dragoons that he has under his command for the city of Orsha and for the parish in case of a need to quell agricultural turmoil, I sent a troop of soldiers to Tolochin. Apart from that, I have suggested the police chief to have a full investigation which will find out about the instigating and leading activity of the people mentioned above to take measures for their arrest.

Acting in lieu of the Governor, vice-governor Ladizhenskiy (Ладыженский), Head of Chancellery.

The years between 1900 and 1936 witnessed the decline of Jewish Tolochin. The mixture of state-sponsored pogroms along with the social unrest that swept the Russian Empire led a large portion of the Jews of

Tolochin to emigrate from the village before the 1917 Russian Revolution. During the interim years between the revolution and World War II, numerous families immigrated to larger cities within the Soviet Union, particularly to Minsk and Moscow. Nevertheless, during the early Soviet period, 106 Jews were craftsmen and 37 families engaged in agriculture. A Yiddish elementary school also operated in Tolochin.

Most of the Jews that fled Tolochin migrated to the United States where they maintained their distinct identities as Tolochiners. These Tolochin immigrants established a "fareng" or organization to help other Tolochiners emigrate to the United States and acculturate to their new homeland. The society, known as the Tolochiner Friends Society, had Harry Paretzky as the first President and was organized officially on December 30, 1914. This society required that its members pay dues and that any person who came from this town could become a member. If a person fell on hard times or didn't have a job, the society would help them. The society also had a form of universal health care. It hired a doctor out of university and the society paid the doctor a stipend and the doctor saw members of the society at a discounted rate. The society made sure to take care of its members who, in many cases, were part of an extended Jewish family with centuries-deep roots in the Tolochin region.[3]

In 1935 and 1936, there was a devastating famine in the region which only prompted further emigration from Tolochin to other regions within the Soviet Union. Reports provided that Jewish villagers were dying in the streets from starvation, with death rates higher than in the pogroms[4]. Oral reports provided that villagers ate dead bodies while the Russian government sent the town's bread to Germany under the Soviet Union's then treaty with the Nazi state.

---

[3] The minutes and records of the society are presently in the possession of Rebecca Grutman Kirkpatrick.
[4] This included members of the extended Rutstein, Paretzky, and Epstein families.

This famine lasted until the Nazi sneak attack against the Soviet Union in 1941. The Nazis occupied Tolochin on July 6, 1941. A ghetto was set up in Tolochin and 2,000 Jews from the town and nearby villages were concentrated there. When the Nazi Einsatzgruppen units entered Tolochin, they directed all the Jews to move to a central location. Then they divided Jews and non-Jews and lined up all the Jews and gypsies into a straight line. The Nazis directed all the Jews to step forward. Many Jews were immediately executed. In the ghetto, many Jews were indiscriminately shot, killed, and raped by their non-Jewish neighbors. The remaining Jews, nearly two thousand, were eventually brought by horse carriage to Raitsy – which is located by the outskirts of Tolochin. In Raitsy, the Nazis (and their local non-Jewish and Crimean collaborators) stripped the remaining Jews of their clothing and marched them naked to what would be their common end in a mass grave. All or most of the Jews of Tolochin were individually and systematically murdered at gunpoint within a day or so of March 13, 1942. The town was liberated by the Red Army in June 1944.

In the 1960s, a memorial was erected at the location of the mass grave. Yuri Dorn, a former head of the Belarus Jewish community, reported that the details of ghetto life and the facts of the Jews' execution were at once time found in the local museum at Pionerskaya ST. 4, which was once under the directorship of Irina Pikulik. The museum is located in the house that, before the war, belonged to a rich Jew, who was an owner of a glass-blowing shop. However, the author visited the museum in 2005, and there was not a single mention of Jewish life before the war or the unique destruction of Tolochin's Jews as part of the Holocaust. It appeared to the author that references to the cities' Jewish pasts was systematically omitted from the museum's official histories of the village.

As of June 1, 2004, 23 Jews lived in Tolochin. All of them are elderly people who lived in mixed Jewish and non-Jewish families. The synagogues were destroyed during World War II – although the building of the local *cheder*, or Jewish school, remains. A functioning pre-war Jewish cemetery is preserved in the town with the assistance of the local Lipshitz family, one of the last remaining Jewish families of the town. The family, until

2000, maintained some portions of the Jewish cemetery out of their personal funds but the cemetery has since fallen into disrepair. The location of the cemetery is to the left of the road from Tolochin to the village of Slobodka. Non-Jewish locals have, in the past few decades, begun to make Christian burials at the cemetery. Part of the cemetery is used for grazing by local shepherds. The author met most of the remaining Jews in 2005, and (nearly) all of them are senior citizens. No doubt, within a short time, the last of the Jews of Tolochin will cease to live thus ending a chapter of a long history of Jews in the village.

PART II

THE PORETZKYN FAMILY: A FAMILY OF TOLOCHIN

Abstract

This history outlines the life of Rabbi Zvi Hirsch Paretzky(n) (1856-1933) and his siblings and children as residents of the village of Tolochin, a small *shtetl* in Central Belarus. The history traces their individual and collective decision to migrate from their homeland to the United States at the turn of the twentieth century and their subsequent acculturation in their new homes in Brooklyn, New York.

The Origin of the Name Poretzkyn

The original surname of the family was Poretzkyn. There are different theories as to the origin of the surname:

1. The surname originated from Perez - a name of many people who escaped from the expulsion of the Jews from Spain and settled in the Russian pale of settlement.
2. According to Ruth Poretsky Hershkovitz, the surname is associated with the name or title "Poret." That term was associated with bourgeoisie status and land ownership in Eastern Europe.
3. Gregory Poretskin states as follows: "what I know about the surname is that in Belarus, there is a place called Porechka, which means "Smordina" in Russian, and translates to a redberry and people that lived in that place had my surname."
4. Along the lines put forth by Gregory Poretskin, Professor Dmitry Shirochin opines that the name Poretzkin is most probably derived from the name "Porech'e" which means "near/of the river" "rechka" = river in Russian. There were, and there are, many villages in Belarus, particularly in Mogilev region, which are called Porech'e. The Yiddish

14

suffix "Kin" connotates belonging to a place or person (i.e. the surname Rivkin 'belonging to Rivka') or in our case, Porechkin, belong to or being of the river.

5. Another theory, put forth by the author, is that Poretzkyn is derived from the surname Berezkin which is a generic non-Jewish surname from the Berezina River near Babruysk.

6. The author opines that the surname could indicate descent from an individual named Peretz and that the 'kin' is the Yiddish suffix indicating "of Peretz."

It's unclear as to why some members of the Moshe Bunim Poretzkyn family started using the name Poretsky/Paretzky/Poret while others retained Paretzkyn/Poretskin/Poretzkyn[5]. The surname has been spelled in a variety manner phonetically, including Poretsky, Poretzky, and Paret. Throughout this document, I intentionally employ different variations of the surname much in the way members of the family did. As of 1875, the surname Poretzkyn was used in public records containing references to this family. It's unclear when the surname Poretzky was adopted but possibly during the 1890s or even upon arrival in the United States.

DNA Analysis

Y-Chromosome DNA testing was conducted on Nathaniel Powers, grandson of Nathan Poretzky, great-grandson of Zvi Hirsch Poretzkyn. Extrapolating his results to all Poretzkyn men reveals that the Poretzkyn men belong to Haplogroup E-M35 also known as E1b1b1. Haplogroup E-M35 accounts for approximately 18% to 20% of Ashkenazi and 8.6% to 30% of Sephardi Y-chromosomes. Its presence among Jews all over the world from Yemen to Europe, from Turkey to Spain, argues geneticists and suggests that

---

[5] Other lines of Poretzkyns originated in Tolochin and were established in the United States and Israel. It is unclear how these lines connect to the Moshe Bunim Poretzkyn family, but it is logical to assume they are related. Those lines include (a) Lev Leib Poretzkyn and Esther Glucko via their son Isaac Mordechai Poretzkyn (born 8/27/1888); and (b) Beila Poretzky, born 1852, immigrated in 1912 with daughter Paja and son Abram and immigrated to Pennsylvania, and another son, Hirsch Poretzky, remained in Tolochin.

Haplotype E–M35 was one of the major founding lineages of the biblical Jewish population. Poretzkyn men are not Kohanim or Levites but are rather Israelites.

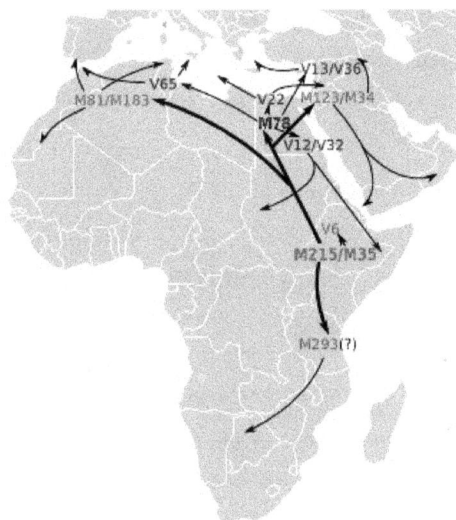

The E–M35 marker is rare among non-Jewish Europeans and is more widespread among Near Eastern populations, many of whom are Arabized and Islamisized, and confirms overwhelmingly the middle eastern origin of the Poretzkyn male line as demonstrated by the above migration chart. Genetically, the Poretzkyn marker clusters most closely with Jewish men from Belarus and more distantly with a small group of Roman, Spanish, and Arab men. Further DNA testing and upgrades are needed to resolve questions regarding the historical migration of this male line and resolve conclusively the origin of the Poretzkyn Y–chromosome.

Geography & Overview of Tolochin, Belarus

Before the Russian Revolution, the Jews of Belarus were forced to live in a region known as "The Pale of Settlement," which spanned from the Baltic Sea to the Black Sea. About 5 million Jews (94% of the total Jewish population, about 12% of the Russian population) lived in this region. The poverty rate was high, and the Jews had the worst jobs, worked for the lowest wages, and in the most demeaning positions. Pogroms occurred frequently throughout the Russian Empire. The Poretzkyn, Rutstein, and Epstein families, who appear to have been closely associated, were concentrated in the region between the city of Minsk and the town of Orsha. These families settled its smaller hamlets or villages, primarily Tolochin.

The Poretzkyn Family Tree in Europe

Little is known about the family genealogical structure as it existed in Europe in the period prior to immigration to the United States. Based on oral

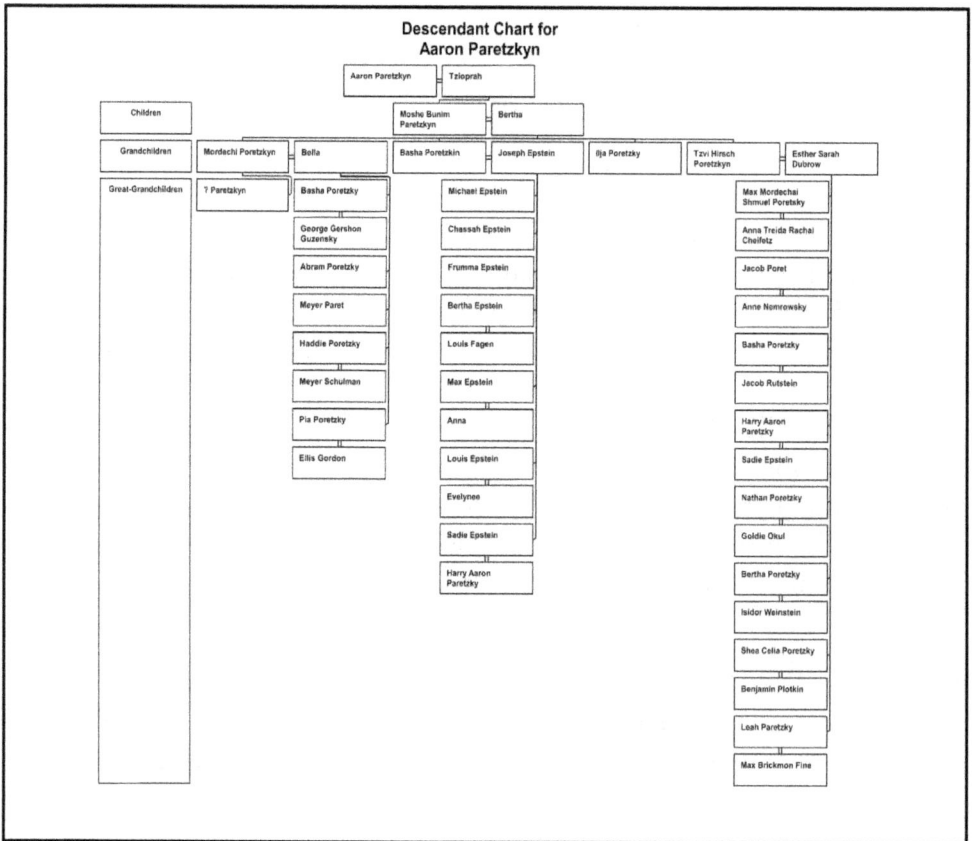

Descendant Chart for Aaron Paretzkyn

Children	Grandchildren	Great-Grandchildren

Aaron Paretzkyn — Tzioprah

Moshe Bunim Paretzkyn — Bertha

Mordechi Poretzkyn	Bella	Basha Poretzkin	Joseph Epstein	Ilja Poretzky	Tzvi Hirsch Poretzkyn	Esther Sarah Dubrow

Great-Grandchildren:

7 Paretzkyn — Basha Poretzky

| Michael Epstein | | Max Mordechai Shmuel Poretzky |

| George Gershon Guzensky | Chassah Epstein | Anna Treida Rachai Cheifetz |

| Abram Poretzky | Frumma Epstein | Jacob Poret |

| Meyer Paret | Bertha Epstein | Anne Nemrowsky |

| Haddie Poretzky | Louis Fagen | Basha Poretzky |

| Meyer Schulman | Max Epstein | Jacob Rutstein |

| Pia Poretzky | Anna | Harry Aaron Paretzky |

| Ellis Gordon | Louis Epstein | Sadie Epstein |

| | Evelynee | Nathan Poretzky |

| | Sedie Epstein | Goldie Okul |

| | Harry Aaron Paretzky | Bertha Poretzky |

| | | Isidor Weinstein |

| | | Shea Celia Poretzky |

| | | Benjamin Plotkin |

| | | Leah Paretzky |

| | | Max Brickmon Fine |

history interviews, we can postulate that at roughly the turn of the twentieth century, the family looked approximately something like the chart above.[6]

The Children of Moshe Bunim & Breina Poretzkyn

The earliest known progenitor of the Poretzkyn family is Moshe Bunim Poretzkyn. Moshe Bunim married Bertha (Breina?)[7]. To them were born at least four children: (1) Isaac[8]; (2) Mordechai; (3) Basha; (3) Ilja[9]; (4) Zvi Hirsch.

Mordechai. Archival records hint that Mordachai Poretzkyn (1854/5 – 19??) may have been one of the elder of the four known children[10]. Research reveals that in 1874/5, Mordechai was drafted into the Russian Army. This event would have been traumatic to Moshe Bunim and Breina who lived through the age of the Cantonist schools, *khappers* (kidnappers), and other discriminatory policies of Czar Nicholas I. From 1827 to 1874, the couple had witnessed children as young as eight years old drafted into the Russian Army for twenty-five-year terms where many of these children suffered from starvation, physical and psychological pressure to convert to Christianity[11]. An example of this is what occurred to Benjamin Epstein, the elder brother of Moshe Bunim's son-in-law, Joseph Epstein. Benjamin had been drafted into the Russian Army as a twelve-year-old boy and served twenty-five years. After the twenty-five years, he came out of the army at the age of 37. Traumatized

---

[6] Some of the marriages represented in this chart occurred in the United States, not Belarus.

[7] Ruth Poretsky Hershkowitz posits that Moshe Bunim's father's name may have been named Aaron, but this cannot be confirmed.

[8] This name is revealed by research. Possible birth date is 1830, but this needs further research.

[9] Archival Research reveals the existence of another son named Ilja Poretzky who appears to have migrated to Ukraine. A 1922 record provides that he lived in Charkov at Mushanka 16/6. Nothing else is known about him.

[10] One of Mordechai's descendants is Gail Gordan Hyamowitz, a Poretzky family researcher. Mordechai had a daughter named Basha Poretzky, sister of Pia Paretzky, who married Gershon Guzinsky, and whose daughter is Gail Gordon. She has documented this line extensively in her family research. When Bessie and Pia immigrated to the United States, they went to stay with their nearest relatives, Hirsch Paretzky.

[11] See Yohanan Petrovsky-Shtern, Jews in the Russian Army, 1827-1917: Drafted into Modernity. Cambridge and New York, Cambridge University Press, 2009.

by the experience, Benjamin sought to regain his faith and begin his life. The family helped him do that by arranging a career and marriage with Moshe Bunim's granddaughter.

Few of the children drafted into the Russian army were able to remain observant Jews during military service, and the majority of those that survived were not as lucky as Benjamin to ever see their families again. The military draft devastated the Jewish community, increased class tensions, eroded confidence in rabbinic leadership, and created a consistent sense of panic among Jewish parents, including Moshe Bunim and Breina, that their children would be taken away from them by the state. Their greatest fears manifested when their son, Mordechai, was drafted into the Russian army in 1875. However, lucky for Mordechai, in 1874, Alexander II engaged in a series of reforms that reduced military service to six years and raised the draft age. After his years of service, Mordechai married a woman named Bella and had three daughters, the first of which, Basya, was born in 1885[12].

Basha. Basha Poretzkyn (1854/5 – 1926) married Yosef Epstein of Orsha in an arranged marriage[13]. Basha left Tolochin to live in Orsha with

------

[12] See infra fn. 15.

[13] The Epstein family was affiliated with Orsha. The Epstein family was part of a much larger Epstein 'tribe' spread throughout the region. Yosef Epstein was said to be the son of Avraham Epstein, the son of Alexander Epstein, the son of Michael Epstein, the son of Moshe Epstein (who is said to have had four different wives) and many, many children. The Epstein's were Levites. The Epstein-Paretzkyn children were:

  a. Michael Epstein, who stayed in Russia and inherited the carrier service business of his father Joseph Epstein. Michael got married and had five children. His children participated in the Russian Revolution, changed their names, and gave up their religion.

  b. Chassah Epstein married her cousin Jacob Epstein. Their fathers were first cousins. They had four children, one died in Russia. Two were born in the United States. The children were: Louis Epstein, Sam Epstein, and Esther Epstein.

  c. Max Epstein had been drafted into the Russian army. He acquired a furlough and the family pooled its resources together. They sold the silverware and the salavare, and they gave it to his wife and shipped him to the United States so he could avoid further military service. Max Epstein was in the construction business who built lower-priced homes. He married a Hannah, and had three boys: Oscar Epstein, Morris Epstein, and Joseph Epstein.

  d. Bertha Epstein had a great singing voice and was very pretty. She married Louis Fagen who was a butcher. Sadie Epstein introduced Louis and Bertha. Louis and Bertha had

Yosef and his family. Although Basha had an arranged marriage, she and Yosef eventually fell very much in love with one another—a love that made a deep and generational impression on their children and grandchildren. Yosef and Basha lived in Orsha on a farm and lived off the produce of the land. They ate red meat only on the holidays. Otherwise during the week, and on Shabbat, they ate fish or chicken, which they raised. They also owned a cow which provided them with a regular supply of milk. Yosef owned a shipping business with his cousin, whose Epstein descendants migrated to Scandinavia.

Yosef and Basha were on good terms and had good relationships with their non-Jewish neighbors. These non-Jewish neighbors reportedly saved her life and those of her children during the pogroms, and raids by the Cossacks by hiding the Epstein-Poretzkyn family in their homes. The couple appeared to have had some disposable cash and were progressive, as they hired private tutors to educate their daughters as there were no schools for Jewish girls at the time in Orsha. The Epstein girls learned to read and write Yiddish, Russian, and French.

Basha and Yosef immigrated with each other to the United States. Ruth Poretzky Hershkowitz remembers Basha Paretzkyn as a short but happy woman who lovingly read to her as a child. Basha wouldn't speak to her children or grandchildren in English but she understood every word. Basha was on excellent terms with her children, and her sons and daughters-in-law loved her and Yosef and would fight among themselves for their attention. After Yosef died, the children and their spouses named their sons after him.

---

a son named Seymour Fagen who lives in Los Angeles, and who at the age of 90 is as fun, vibrant, and dynamic as a man of 30.

    e.   Louis Epstein was a lawyer. He married Rose Epstein (no relation) who was introduced to him by her brother, who was his classmate in law school. They had two children: Judy and an unknown boy Epstein.

    f.   Frumma Epstein was the oldest daughter. She married her uncle, Benjamin Epstein. Benjamin had served in the Russian army. He had been drafted as a twelve-year old boy into the service and the term of service was twenty-five years. After twenty-five years, he came out of the army at the age of 37. The youngest daughter of Joseph wanted to get married and Benjamin wanted to begin his life, so they arranged the marriage.

    g.   Sadie Epstein, who married her first cousin, Harry Paretzky.

Yosef died of a burst appendix in a hospital. Everyone blamed the hospital for his death. As a result, many in the Epstein family were skeptical of hospitals, thus, Sadie Epstein gave birth to her daughter, Ruth[14], at home.

Zvi Hirsch. Zvi Hirsch Poretzkyn (1856 – 1922) was born in approximately 1856 or 1857 in the vicinity of Tolochin, Belarus. He was called Hirsch and Girsch in official records. As a young man, Zvi Hirsch received rabbinic ordination and presumably studied in a Yeshiva—although it is not known which one. Rabbi Zvi Hirsch was reputed to be a learned and wise man, a great Torah scholar, a *Talmud chochom*, and a *tzaddik*. He was referred to as the/a "Rav" of Tolochin, who mediated disputes between individuals. In his youth, he had been referred to as a "nativ kest." The system of the *nativ kest* was practiced by the Jews of Tolochin. The shtetl Jews were motivated by the Torah-inspired value that it was more important to marry a daughter to a Torah scholar than to a rich man. In most instances, the parents of a wealthy daughter would take the smart and educated young men and marry their child to him. Apparently, Zvi Hirsch was one of those young and scholarly men.

Zvi Hirsch married Esther Sarah Dubrow, the daughter of Avraham Elitzur Dubrow and Sima (Sylvia) Fagen. Esther Sarah was also born in Tolochin on March 3, 1861. The marriage was arranged. Together, the couple established/owned an inn, shop, and dairy farm. Their family owned a barn and cows and was engaged in some sort of small-scale agricultural farming. Esther Sarah Dubrow was deemed a "baalabusta" as she was the one who primarily managed the inn and ran the dairy farm.

Tolochin, being a border town at the time (some say near the main travel route), had many travelers who stop and spend the night. The family, and inn, was a proud owner of a seltzer machine. This high-tech machine was a good investment and provided the family with good financial returns and additional income. Before the World War I and the Russian Revolution, the business was profitable enough to allow Zvi Hirsch to focus on his rabbinic

---

[14] Ruth Poretsky, daughter of Aaron Poretzky, was named Rivka after her mother's grandmother.

studies. Zvi Hirsch was thus able to become the author of many manuscripts on a variety of subjects, including Torah, Talmud, and Halacha. Unfortunately, all of these works have been lost to history[15]._According to Ruth Poretzky Hershkovitz, "Esther Sarah ran the inn, and Hirsch did not work with his hands, he worked with his head. Esther Sarah was a breadwinner and had strong business acumen. Zvi Hirsch wasn't expected to dirty his hands to make a living." Rather, Zvi Hirsch was the "village's wise man" and scholar. He would lead prayers and teach in the synagogue. Yet despite his communal duties, Zvi Hirsch was reported to be simultaneously a shopkeeper and wheat broker

The Children of Zvi Hirsch Paretzkyn & Esther Sarah Dubrow

The couple had at least twelve children together. The lives of Zvi Hirsch's children were heavily shaped by the official policy of the Russian Empire towards its Jewish population as crafted by the Czar's procurator of the Holy Synod, Constantine Pobedonostev. The policy entailed that "one-third of the Jews should be expelled, one-third should convert to Christianity, and one-third should be killed."

This policy was somewhat effective concerning the Poretzkyn family. Four of Zvi Hirsch's children were murdered through this policy and the rest were exiled. Based on oral history accounts, the author posits that one child died/was killed in infancy, two were killed in pogroms (possibly when boarding a train running for their lives from anti-Semitic mobs), and one from disease/famine. Only the names of the eight surviving children are known.

The children of Zvi Hirsch and Esther Poretzky were:

1. Mordechai Shmuel Max (b. 1878)
2. Basha "Basya" Bessie (b. March 1885/1888)
3. Yaakov "Yankel" Jacob (b. March 16, 1887)
4. Aaron "Ahra" Harry (b. January 15, 1893)

---

[15] The author believes some reference to his work may be preserved at YIVO Institute.

5. Noach Nachum Nathan (b. 1894)
6. Breta Breina Bertha (b. January 2, 1900/1902)
7. Tziporah "Shea" Celia (b. July 1, 1904)
8. Leah Lillian (b. 1905)
9. Unknown
10. Unknown
11. Unknown
12. Unknown

Most of the biographical details in the lives of these individuals arise in the context of the pogroms and other forms of persecution. The pogroms were a series of raids and riots against the local Jewish population. They occurred from the 1820s through 1935 and culminated in the Holocaust (1939-1945). The pogroms were organized attempts by local and national authorities to massacre and harass the Jews. According to Ruth Poretzky Hershkovitz, the Cossacks would periodically ransack, raid, pillage, and rape the Jews of Tolochin. The local Jews would run from village to village and hide with friends or in the forests. These pogroms, often state-sponsored, were one of the primary motivations of Jewish families leaving the former Russian Empire, including the Poretzkyn family. It prompted numerous different branches of the family to migrate to the United States and elsewhere.

During the pogroms, the sons of Esther Dubrow and Rabbi Zvi Hirsch Poretzkyn would help their sisters climb into barrels and then cover them with apples and potatoes, or on other occasions, huddle them behind the tapestries which covered the walls or help them into the cellars. It was done to prevent their sisters from being raped by Cossacks and their non-Jewish neighbors.

Basha, being the oldest girl, some say the oldest child, helped her mother Esther take care of the other children and different arms of the family businesses. Basha, as a result, never received any formal education, something she felt terrible about for the rest of her life. According to her son, Milton Rothstein, "Bessie never had the education the rest of her family had. She worked in the tea house owned by grandfather and raised the many younger children, mostly her sisters." Rita Kaplan, her daughter, relates that Basha ran away from home and hid among a pile of coals because the family would not let her go to school as a child because she was the (older) girl. Bessie was subsequently found, but her act of protest did not result in her obtaining an education.

Charity or Tzedaka was a central value in the Poretzkyn-Dubrow household. Basha was raised with daily examples of such charity. A saying of Rabbi Zvi Hirsch that has been passed onto Basha was, "it is better to give *tsedaka* [charity] to nine fakers that don't deserve than to turn away one who does." Bessie took her father's teaching to a new level and gave charity, food, and clothing to all who asked. People said to her, "you are giving money to worthless fakers." She would reply, "If I gave to 9 fakers and only one is a deserving charity, then I am satisfied." Bessie was good-hearted and gave to all charities and beggars. She bought fruit from the peddlers and poor (just) to help them. According to Milton Rothstein, Basha's son, "she was a loving decent slave to her family" in Europe and in the United States. According to Ruth Paretzky Hershkovitz, Basya (Bessie) had an arranged marriage while still in Tolochin when she was seventeen or eighteen years old. Basha is said to have known her future husband in Tolochin, Belarus but only became romantically involved when she fled her "slavery" in Russia."

In or around 1901, Aaron, who was then approximately eleven years old, returned from playing with his friends (or hunting) out in the fields of Tolochin. Aaron found that his family and other members of the community had been herded by (local) mobs into the synagogue. The mob locked the Jews locked inside the synagogue and lit the building on fire. Aaron, along with his friends who had also been playing in the fields, broke open the doors of the synagogue and freed their family and neighbors. The synagogue subsequently was burned to the ground. This was a defining moment in Aaron's life, and at that moment, he later recalled, he became a Zionist. It was likely around this time, that Aaron was sent to Minsk and apprenticed to a cousin who was a baker. Aaron had been sent along with his brother Nathan to learn the baking trade from this cousin.

Up to four of the Poretzkyn children were murdered in the pogroms. According to Bonnie Brody, "2-4 siblings were killed [by mobs while] boarding the train leaving Tolochin." It's not clear if only part of these four or all four were killed boarding the train of Tolochin or whether some were killed in other pogroms and others while boarding the train.

By all accounts, life for the Poretzkyn family was difficult. By 1900, it appears that some family members considered leaving Tolochin. Positive reports about life in America coupled with state-sponsored antisemitism and pogroms against the Jewish community were factors in favor of the family deciding to leave[16]. One source provides that Mordechai Shmuel, being the eldest, was the first to emigrate to the United States and did so as early as 1900 or 1901—perhaps as a result of the Tolochin Pogrom of 1900. Another account provides that Mordechai Shmuel immigrated with his younger brother, Yankel, in 1906. Official records have not been able to resolve this discrepancy.

Pressure on Jews to leave Belarus increased drastically between 1903 and 1905 when a series of larger pogroms swept the region and led to the death and maiming of many Jews. At the same time, the draft which demanded an extended military service, during an active war with the Empire of Japan, along with the repugnance of serving an empire which actively persecuted Jews and the Poretzkyn family, led the family and many other Jews to consider permanent migration.

According to Ruth Paretzky Hershkovitz, Yankel was the first, along with Mordechai Shmuel, to depart to the United States. According to another source, Jacob is reported to have arrived either in 1904 or 1906. In or around the same time, Yankel Poretzkyn was drafted into the Russian Army.

---

[16] This may have been earlier. Some reports indicate that family members arrived as early as 1902. It's possible that Max and Jacob Poret predated the arrival of Jacob Rutstein who is known to have immigrated in 1905. According to one narrative, Max and Jacob Poretzkyn arrived in 1900. According to some accounts, Max and Jacob Poret were simultaneously joined by Nathan and Basha (Bessie) but others say that these two came after Max and Jacob Poret. Three possible dates exist for Nathan's arrival: 1905, 1906, and 1909.

Unwilling to dedicate his life to a state which did not offer him the benefits of citizenship, Jacob fled to the United States. Deserting the draft was a crime for which the government would engage in collective punishment against the family financially and otherwise. However, despite this, the Poretzkyn family came together and braced themselves for that retaliation.

Upon arrival in the United States at the age of 17, Yankel Poretzkyn's surname was changed to Poret based upon an act of an immigration official and Yankel became Jacob. When Jacob first arrived in the United States, he had the equivalent of $10 in his pocket. Jacob's first job was as a bricklayer. Mordechai Shmuel became Max and he adopted the surname Paretzky. It is not known what career Max first did upon arrival, but he too eventually worked in the real estate industry as a builder. According to the history compiled by Bonne Brodie, the siblings "first lived at 316 E. 7th Street, Brooklyn, N.Y. The family would stay with Max because he had hot water. Max was a builder or ran a lumberyard and liked to play cards."

Noach Nathan reportedly left Belarus because he had killed someone in self-defense during a pogrom (or was a revenge killing later in retaliation for the violence done against his family during a pogrom) and was afraid of being retaliated against in return. Records also provide that he was later drafted into the military.

Sometime between 1905 to 1906, Basha arrived in the United States. Jacob sent her a ticket, so she traveled with her brother (not clear which one) to the United States. According to one account, when Basha arrived in the United States, she at first didn't recognize her future husband, who she had known in Tolochin, because he had remade himself into the likes of a 'European gentlemen.' One can imagine all of the siblings dressed in the wares of the shtetl only to remake themselves in America. As soon as she was able, Basha, who became known as Bessie, enrolled in night school to get the education she could not get in Europe.

In 1907, the siblings were eventually joined by Aaron, the youngest of the boys who had been living in a house filled with women in Europe with his sisters. Ruth Hershkovitz describes the feeling of the siblings, particularly of Nathan and Harry, of coming to the United States: "They came to America and they were free—especially after how they lived in Russia with the pogroms and everything. For the first time, they were free, they were free of their parents, they were free of the Jewish laws, and they didn't have to obey somebody. They were on their own. And they made it. But the one thing they had was that they had been taught a trade. They were both bakers. Nathan was a cake maker and Aaron made fancy bread." The two would eventually open up a bakery together.

According to Ruth Hershkovitz, in or around 1907, Aaron arrived on the ship Leviathan to the United States when he was approximately fourteen years old. Tziporah Sadie (Zlateh) Epstein, his cousin and future wife, arrived a year later on the same ship. Aaron was a stowaway on the Leviathan. Aaron had a friend whose family had twelve children and decided to go with them. However, when Aaron arrived in the United States at Castle Gardens (which is where immigrants arrived prior to Ellis Island), his friend's family denied knowing him because they didn't want to be financially responsible for him. Aaron was to be deported but he told the immigration officials that he had brothers in the United States. The brothers were beckoned, and Max and Jacob signed an affidavit stating they would be responsible for Aaron. When Aaron arrived in New York, he was renamed Harry by an immigration official. According to Ruth Hershkovitz, Aaron, or Harry as he was now called, was completely on his own in America. Aaron had been away from home before. Yet nothing in his life could prepare him for navigating the new world alone while his parents remained in Europe, and his older brothers struggled to establish the family in the United States.

Should the siblings have any doubt about their ability to return to the land of their birth, two announcements from 1909 in a Mogilev province newspaper show that such an option was impossible. The records provide that Orsha county police department was looking for Yankel (the son of Hirsch) Poretzkyn and his siblings Mordukh Shmuila, Noach, Aron, and Basya. The announcement provides that Yankel Paretzkyn was drafted into the military in 1906 but did not appear. A subsequent announcement provides that the Orsha County police department was looking for Noach (the son of Hirsch)

Poretzkyn and his siblings, Mordukh Shmuila and Basya. The announcement provides that Noach Poretzkyn was drafted by the military in 1907 but did not appear. It is likely around this time period that Rabbi Tzvi Hirsch and Esther were hit with massive fines for their children's evasion of military service. This no doubt contributed to the economic downturn Zvi Hirsch and Esther experienced in the coming decade.

The Poretzky Children Establish Roots in America

Whatever the order the siblings immigrated, and whatever their exact personal motivations for leaving Belarus, or the exact circumstances of their arrival in the United States, three photos between approximately 1909 and 1913 show that Max Poretzky, Harry Paretzky, Jacob Poret, Jacob and Bessie Rutstein, and Nathan Paretzky were in the United States, and that the first grandchildren of Zvi Hirsch and Esther Sarah had been born too. In 1912, at the age of 55, Rabbi Poretzky visited/immigrated to the United States but, for whatever reason, decided to return to Tolochin.

Bessie Paretzky and Jacob Rutstein. Brooklyn, New York. Circa 1909.

From Left to Right: Rabbi Zvi Hirsch Poretzky(n), Max Poretzk), Jacob Poret, Jacob Rutstein, Nathan Poretzky. Brooklyn, New York. Circa 1912.

From top Left to Right standing: Anna and Max Poretsky, Nathan Poretzky, Anna Poret, Bessie Poretzky Rutstein. Middle row from left to right, sitting: Rabbi Zvi Hirsch Poretzky(n), Jacob Poret with infant son Frank Poret, Jacob Rutstein. Row of children from left to right: unknown, unknown, Sidney Poretzky? Nicky Rutstein, Bertha Rutstein. Brooklyn, New York, circa 1913.

Tolochiner Friends Association

During the first decade of the century, the Paretzky brothers and Bessie worked hard to establish themselves in America. Some of the Paretzky siblings and cousins went to create and support a 'fareng' or organization to help other Tolochiners emigrate to the United States and acculturate to their new homeland. The brothers, along with others from the village, formed the Tolochiner Friends Society, whose President was Harry Paretzky. The society was organized officially on December 30, 1914. It required that its members pay dues and that any person who came from this town could become a member. If a person fell on hard times or didn't have a job, the society would help them. It also had a form of universal health care. It hired a doctor out of university and paid the doctor a stipend. The doctor saw members of the society at a discounted rate. The society made sure to take care of its members who, in many cases, were part of an extended Jewish family with centuries deep roots in the Tolochin region. Two brothers of Jacob Rutstein (who married Bessie), Nathan and Sam Rutstein, were also members. Benjamin Plotkin, who would later marry into the Paretzky family, was also a member.[17]

Zionist Harry Fights for A Jewish State in Palestine

Upon his arrival, Harry worked for his brothers for some time. Then, in or around 1916 or 1917, Harry went with a friend to Montana because the two unsupervised teenage boys had decided that they were going to be sheep ranchers. When the Balfour Declaration was declared, Harry, recalling the persecutions of his youth, and being a proud Zionist and Jew, crossed the border into Canada and joined Allenby's brigade with the hope of eventually establishing a Jewish State in the Land of Israel.

Harry Paretzky, Allenby's Brigade, Palestine. Circa 1916.

During his military service, Harry served in Alexandria and Palestine. When Harry was slated to come home, he contracted malaria and ended up in a hospital in Italy. He survived and arrived back in New York in 1920 where he subsequently married his first cousin, Sadie Epstein.

Harry Paretzky. Allenby Brigade. Palestine 1916-1917.

---

[17] The minutes and records of the society are presently in the possession of Rebecca Grutman Kirkpatrick.

Rabbi Poretzky & the Youngest Girls Fend for Themselves in Russia

Zvi Hirsch, Esther Sarah, Bertha, Shea, and Leah remained behind in Tolochin, including through the first world war and the Russian Revolution. The four other unnamed children, murdered by local non-Jews in the pogroms, had presumably remained too. Shea Poretzky related one instance running away from her home to a shelter after the Cossacks burned their barn in a pogrom. Shea grabbed the Samovar and (Breina) Bertha let the cows out of the barn so the cows would survive and not be burned alive.

During the First World War, all the boys had already left Russia. They left behind their three younger sisters and their parents. The Germans came to the village and burned it down. This was reported to have occurred in or around 1917. However, relative to what was to come to the Jews of Tolochin at the hands of the Russians with the creation of the Soviet Union, the Germans were reported to have been relatively nice to the Jews. When the First World War was over, the Russian Revolution started. The Russian peasants didn't care to restrain themselves in their hatred of the Jews. They started raping and pillaging in the Jewish villages. The girls, on one occasion, hid behind a long carpet that had been hanging on the wall to keep the house neat and warm. They did this to avoid being raped by the Russian soldiers and peasants. The girls, with their elderly parents, fled from house to house and then village to village to escape the mayhem created by antisemitic mobs. At the same time, famine and drought devastated the region and many in Tolochin and its vicinity starved to death, including relatives of the family.

Rabbi Zvi Hirsch "Harris" Poretzkyn and Esther Sarah Dubrow. Tolochin, Belarus. Circa 1920.

Letter from Zvi Hirsch Poretzky to Children in America

The following is a letter sent from Tolochin, Belarus, or its vicinity by Zvi Hirsch to Bessie and Jacob Rothstein asking for more information regarding their lives and the lives of their siblings in the New World. The letter references the engagement of Aaron Poretzky and Sadie Epstein and therefore dates the letter to sometime between 1918 and 1920. It is littered with Talmudic sayings and reveals the author to be an educated and literary man. The cursive handwriting, however, is difficult to read and written with a rushed and unsteady hand, which made its transcription and translation very difficult and expensive.

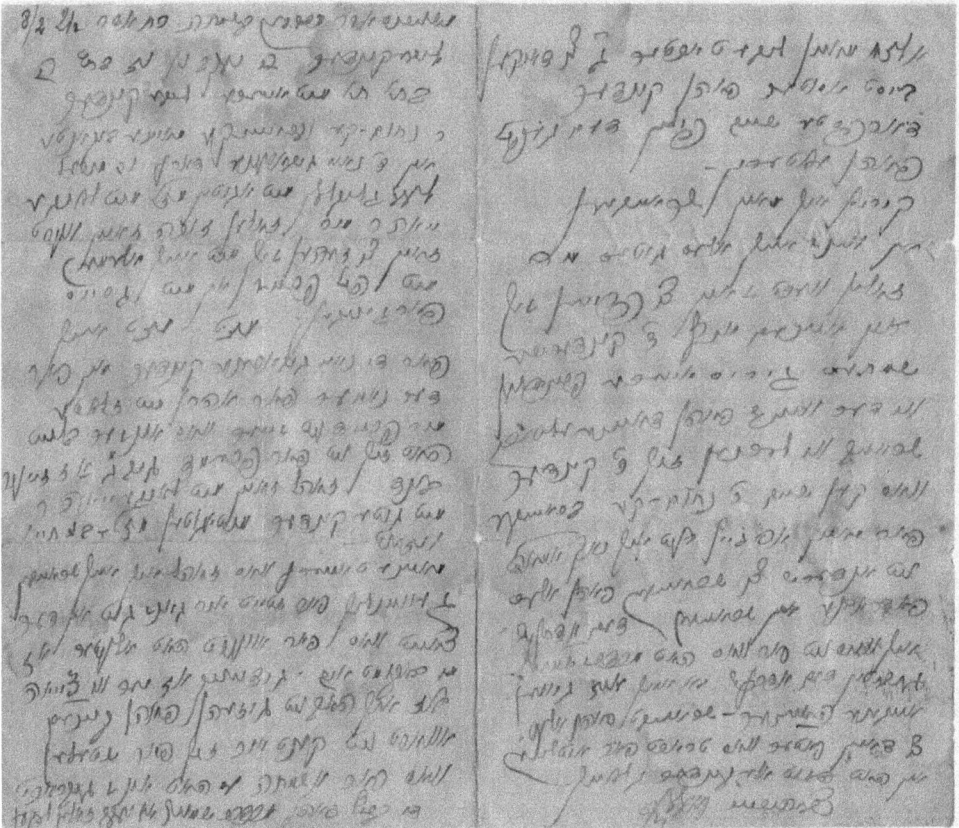

Letter from Tzvi Hirsch Poretzkyn to his children. Tolochin, Belarus.
Circa 1920.

Due to its great significance, I reproduce the whole letter with its Yiddish-English translation as follows:

Yiddish | **English**

בס״ד

אדר כח בשמחה מרבים אדר משנכנס
2\2 2\8

מיט ית בתי. יני יעקבען קינדער ליבע
קע-נחום ר קינדער ליבע אייערע
די אין באקאנטע מאיינע ובראייינקע
גליקלעך לעב זיי - דארף געבאארענע נאיי
מיר יאהר לאנגע מיט מזל גוטען א מיט
זעהען צו זאיין ווערט זאיין זוכה זאלען
פרייד פיל מיט אלעמען אייך מיט גיך
טי״מז טי״מז. פארגעעניגען גרויס מיט און
און קינדער גיבאארענע נאיי די פאר אייך
זלאטע מיט אהרן פאר נייער דער פאר פאר
אונזער וואס זייער דאם פרייד מיר
ג גיב. פרעמד פאר ניט זיך האט בליט
לייננע מיט זאיין זאהל קינד זייער אז
מזל גוטען מיט קינדער גוטע מיט יאהר
ומזוני חיי בני

אייך איך זאהל וואס טייערען מאיינע
איר פארשטייט געוויינלעך שראייבען
פאר וואס צאיית דער אין גוט גאנז
באקומט ווי אז אלעטער האט אווערט
איך אז -צוואה ווי מער איז גידענק. איך
ווארט א קיינעם פאהן גיזעהן ניט האב
וואס פארשטעלען זיך איר קענט ניט
געבראכט אונז האט עס שמחה א פאר
יעקב און שמואל מרדכי פאהן בריף די
לעבען זאלען

With God's help

When the month of Adar arrives, we increase our joy[18]. 28 Adar 2/2 2/8

Dearest children, Yaakov and Bessie and your beloved children R' Nachumke and Braynke, who I know, and the children born recently, may they all live long in happiness and prosperity! May we be granted the chance to see each other soon with great joy and great pleasure! Mazal tov, congratulations to you on the children born recently and the new couple Aharon and Zlateh. We are so happy that we are still close and in contact. May God grant their children long lives with good children and good fortune — children who will survive childhood and prosper[19].

My dearest, what shall I write to you? Surely you understand how much the letters I receive are worth to me. In our times, thinking of one another is more valuable than an inheritance of great fortune, and I have not received a word from either of you. So, you can imagine what joy the letter from Mordechai Shmuel and Yaakov brought us, long may they live.

---

[18] See B. Talmud, tractate Taanit 29a.
[19] See B. Talmud Talmud tractate Moed Qatan, 28a.

33

בתי וועסט דו ליינען איבער מרדכי
שמואלס לעטער וועסטו זעהן וואס זיי
ארבעטין די גאנצע גישעפטין אונזערע
איך האב אין זאיין לעטער אויס
גישריבען איך ווייל מיט דער פאצ'ט ווי
איז באווסט אז איך בין אקרעמער
געוואונליך און שרייב איך אין קראך
גייט דער אכין און אין 2ער2ער אלזא
פאר קיריץ אייך איך רעכען אז מרדכי
שמואלס לעטער איז פאר אלעמען
גישריבען גיווארען אלזא – בלאייבט נאר
איינס אז מיר זאהל זעהן צו שרייבען
און ניט זארגט אונזער גוטער און
גרויסער ג'לעבט און פארלאזט ניט קיין
מענשין איך האף צו אים אז ער וועט ניט
פארלאזען אויף וואייטער .ביז האיינט
זאיינען מיר מיט אלעס זאט –דער
צערות איז אפשר גרייס 1000 אפונט
לחם 3000 פלייש נאר אונזער ג'איז גוט
אז ער קען אין הונגער אויך קארמענען צו
זאיט

מיינע ליבע יעקב און בתל

דארפט איר בעטין ניט אייך דארף איך
אלעס שרייבען און פארשטיין אליין
אז אדרעס אייער געבען און פאדראבנע
אדאנק - שרייבען גלייך זאהל איך
ער לעבען זאהל שמואל מרדכי
און אלעס פאהן ער שרייבט שרייבט
אלעמען פאהן .

שמעון דאיין פאהן שרייבט ער
מיר אבער שמואל נחם פאהן עטליכה
וואלט מיר ווייניק אלעס נאך דאס איז
איטליכען פאהן זעהן און וויסען זיך
צו האנט זייערע מיט באזונדער
אז און אליין שרייב אלזא .שרייבען
די ווי אהרונען און נחם זעהן זיי אז דו
מיין פאהן זיי בעטין עלטערע א ביסט
זייערע טאהן דאס זאלין זיי אז נחומען

Bessie, if you read though Mordekhai Shmuel's letter you will read about their work, and about all our affairs. I described in his letter, as you know, that I am an ordinary shopkeeper and I also wrote that the business is going bankrupt and secondly, secondly [20], in short, I believe that Mordekhai Shmuel's letter was written to everyone. Writing is all we have left – and do not worry, our good and great God lives and does not forsake anyone. I hope that He will not forsake us in the future. Until now we have had everything we needed. There is great hardship [here]; a pound of bread costs more than 1000 and [a pound of] meat more than 3000. Only our God is so great that even in times of [famine and] hunger, He also fills our pockets.

My dear Yaakov and Bessel,

I should not need to ask you, you should understand alone, to write all the details and give your address so that I can write to you immediately. Thanks to Mordekhai Shmuel, may he live long! He writes, he writes about everything and everyone.

He writes some news about your Shimon about Nachum Shmuel, but it is still not enough for me. I want to hear about and read people's news in their own hand. So write yourselves, you will understand, Nachum and Aharon, when you are parents yourself. We ask, my Nachum – that you do this for your old parents, do them the

20 Not a copy error.

צו פארגינוגען דעם עלטערען אלטע
מיר אז געבען וועט ג׳ ביז שראייבען
.איינעם אין קלאייבען איין זיך וועלען
צו ג׳ אלע שוועסטער די מוטער די
זיי פריינדליך און גיריסין דאנקען
זאיינען זיי שראייבען אויך אליין וועלען
פארנומענע

אלזא מאיין ליבע טאכטער ג ׳צו דאנקען
ביסט א מוטער פאהן קינדער דארפסטע
שיים פילען דעם געפיל פאהן עלטערין .
קוריץ אין מאיין שראייבען איך ווינש אייך
אלעס גוטעס מיר זאלין ווערט זאיין צו
פרייען גיך אין איינעם אויף די קינדערישע
שמחות .גיריס אלעמן פריינדליך וי דער
וויס פאהן דאיינע עלטערן שראייב ווי
לערנען זיך די קינדער וואס קען שיים ר ׳
נחום קע וברא אייניקע פאר מאיין אפגיין בעט
איך נאך א מאהל ניט אנדארש צו שראייבען
פאהן אלעס פאדראבנע און שראייבען דעם
אדרעס איך וויס ניט פאר וואס האט מרדכי
שמואל געבעטין דעם אדרעס וו אויך איז
גיוועזן אייגענע האייזער – שראייבט פאהן
אלעס צו דאיין פאטער וואס טראכט פאר
איטליכען און האט האלט אלע אלע קינדער
גלייך

kindness of writing until God reunites us.
Your mother and sister both send warm and
loving greetings, thank God, they will write
themselves, they are busy.

So, my dear daughter, thank God you are
already a mother. You must already have
the feeling of what it is to be a parent. My
letter is brief. I wish you all the best, may
we celebrate together soon at the happy
occasions of the children. Your parents send
loving regards to everyone. Write how and
what the children are learning, what can R.
Nachumke and Braynke do?

Before I finish, I ask you once more to write
about everything, in detail and send your
address. I don't know why Mordekhai
Shmuel asked for the address they were
free-standing houses. Write about
everything to your father who thinks of
each one of you and loves all his children
equally!

Signature (Zvi Hirsch Poretsky)

The Brothers Bring Their Parents & Sisters to America

During World War I, and then during the subsequent Russian Revolution, communication between the siblings in America and their family in Belarus was limited. The brothers in America were very worried about their sisters and their parents. The siblings had a hard time finding them in the chaos, pogroms, and famines then ravaging the collapsing Russian Empire and, for a period, lost contact with them. The siblings, desperate, petitioned the American Red Cross for help. With their help, the sisters and their parents were eventually found. After communication was reestablished with the sisters, Hirsch and Esther Sarah, the Poretzky brothers sent first-class tickets for their sisters and parents. They departed from the port of Libau on a ship named The Lithuania. Because the brothers in America were able to send first-class tickets for their parents and sisters, the girls would not have to shave their heads like the second- or third-class passengers. The girls even purchased some fur coats with the money the brothers had sent them. However, the coats were stolen during their journey. The girls and the parents arrived in New York on May 24, 1922.

According to Sylvia Weinstein, when Hirsch arrived in the United States, he did so with a whole box of rubles. Hirsch was convinced that the Czar would return to power and that the rubles would be valuable. When the three youngest Poretzky girls arrived in the United States, they went to work in the factories. Bertha sewed fancy children's dresses and is reported to have been an excellent seamstress[21]. Shea was a 'rabble-rouser' and tried to start a union in the factory where she worked. Leah eventually became a forelady in the factory where she worked. The brothers took upon themselves to rent a house for their parents and sisters on Ditmus Ave in Brooklyn and then later at 3030 Brighton 12th St, Brooklyn, NY 11235, USA.

Rabbi Zvi Hirsch was a very respected scholar in Brooklyn. Every Friday night, he would sit in the living room, and people would come to him

---

[21] In one photograph, Sylvia, Edie and Harris Weinstein are on a sofa, Sylvia is wearing a yellow dress and Edie is wearing a pink dress that Bertha made using the skills she learned in the factory where she worked.

and ask for advice on halachic questions and discuss their personal issues. Rabbi Hirsch was an avid writer and wrote editorials and essays for the Yiddish newspaper called *Der Tug*, which means "The Day" in Yiddish. Rabbi Zvi Hirsch was also reputed to have written several books in the United States but their whereabouts are unknown or lost[22].

In America, like in Europe, Charity Began at Home:

Family Helped One Another

The oral history from this period reveals how close this family was to one another and how they helped one another. It was this ethic that allowed the group as a whole to get ahead and accomplish their family and financial goals.

One story related by Marty Poretskin illustrates this value. In or around this time, a tragedy occurred to cousins of the Poretzkyn children. In Tolochin, a relative of Zvi Hirsch, Chaim Poretzkyn, and his wife Rachel Altschutz and eight children[23] decided to emigrate to America. Chaim

---

[22] Hank Plotkin says he saw the books. They were bound handwritten notebooks, big and thick. They went with the family from Brooklyn to Allentown, PA. Hank writes, "I remember seeing them in my parents' house on Livingstone Street. I understand my mother gave away all my books and other stuff to Sylvia and Edie when she moved to Florida. I doubt if my mother thought the books were significant to anybody—she could have thrown them out." Sylvia Weinstein says the basement of her home was cleared out when her mother died in 1983. Old Yiddish books (but no manuscripts) were donated to Sons of Israel and Temple Beth El of Allentown, PA. A future family researcher should contact the synagogues to see if some manuscripts were inadvertently donated.

[23] Chaim Paretzkyn was the son of Mordechai Leib Poretzkyn (who was said to have been married two or three times) and was a relative of Tzvi Hirsch. The author posits that Chaim was the great-nephew of Tzvi Hirsch and that Mordechai Leib is the same as Mordechai, the son of Moshe Bunim, mentioned above. The author bases this on the 1922 ship manifest of Chaim's children emigration to the United States. The children listed Hirsch Poretzkyn of Orsha as their Uncle. The author posits that Chaim Poretzkyn (1873 – 1922) was born to the first marriage of Mordechai Leib Poretzkyn. The other children born to Mordechai, the line researched by Gail Haymowitz, are a product of his second marriage posits the author.

According to Lisa Kerner, Mordechai Leib and his best friend arranged the marriage between Chaim and Rachel Altshutz. Rachel was the second of 16 children. "The two men were good friends. Both were observant Jews and both co-owners of a butcher shop. The two friends felt that their children would make them proud grandparents." According to Linda Appleman Shapiro, "Chaim was a mediator. When problems occurred in the neighborhood, Chaim would step in and advise... Anyone

Poretzkyn left his family and immigrated to the United States and migrated to Wilkes-Barre, Pennsylvania and prepared for his family to immigrate. Over time, Rachel and her children sorted, sold, and donated their assets in preparation for their immigration to the United States. Just as the family was about to leave, Rachel died. The pre-teenage children, who were homeless and starving, managed to get themselves onto the ship to the United States. When they arrived in the United States, however, they learned that their father, Chaim, had died too. The children found themselves in a strange new country, alone, with no parents, and without knowing the language and nobody to take care of them.

The Poretzkyn family in America came together to help the children. The Poretzkyn siblings also came together in their own way to assist their cousins to recover from this tragedy. Some of the orphaned children went to live with their uncle and aunt Basha Poretzkyn and her husband Moshe Frotkin. Basha and Moshe didn't have any of their own children. However, when they came to the United States, they adopted several of Chaim's children and their nephews and nieces, as their own children after the loss of the children's parents. Basha and Moshe tried their best to instill their nephews and nieces with Jewish values and education. They tried to prevent the assimilatory habits of Jewish immigrants to this country and help them preserve their Jewish identity.

According to Gail Gordon and Ethel Poretzky, the Rutstein-Poretsky house on President street was, on occasion, a reunion center for the extended

---

that couldn't afford the meat at the butcher store, Chaim would give them pieces of meat for free. He was the type of man that he would lend a hand whenever he could." Chaim liked to grow his own vegetables in his yard and every Friday before Shabbas, he would take them and distribute them to poor peasants. After Rachel died, their children took their mother's body home from the hospital on a sled and dragged it in the cold to the house to perform the rites of the body. Chaim and Rachel had the following children: Elie Paretzkyn, Pauline Paretzkyn, Miriam Paretzkyn, Abe Poretzkyn, Bessie Poretskin, Leah Poretksin, and Yitzchok Poretskin. They all married and had children, and their descendants live throughout the United States. More about this branch of the family can be found in Linda Appleman Shapiro's book "She's Not Herself."

family. Ethel Poretzky remembers going to visit Jacob and Bessie and their children. Marty Poretzkyn also remembers visiting the family at the Rutstein house on President's Street at a family get together and that it was a really nice house. However, for the most part, the family gathered at the home of Rabbi Zvi Hirsch Poretzkyn and Esther Sarah in the Flatbush area of Brooklyn on Ditmas Avenue and 4th Street, which was on top of a hardware store. Jacob Poret owned the apartment that Leah, Hirsch, Esther Sarah, and the other girls lived in, and together they lived there for free. Many of the grandchildren of Esther Sarah can recall her sitting outside of the apartment reading the *tzenehrena* prayers, which are Yiddish prayers authored by and for women. On Shabbas, Esther Sarah would sit on the patio all day and *daven* or pray for her family, children, husband, and the end of all human suffering.

Bertha was the first of the youngest daughters to marry and leave the house on Ditmus Avenue. Bertha married Isadore Weinstein. She and "Izzy," as he was affectionately known, moved out to another apartment. Harmon Brody described Izzy Weinstein as follows: "Isadore Weinstein was perhaps the most generous and charitable man of all. He built the first temple in Allentown, Pennsylvania. He would give you the very shirt off of his back and so would his wife Bertha. Isadore would hire black garment workers when nobody else would. Bertha would send food along with them [to the workers] even before the ILGWU (Union) existed. Isadore Weinstein would not fire his workers because they needed to take care of their families. Izzy Weinstein was a great man and was idealized by so many. He took care of the community. I met this man. He is a historical character."

Hank Plotkin swelled up in tears when he talked about Izzy and said that describing Izzy Weinstein as "generous" was an understatement. Izzy completely changed Hank's life and was like a father to him. Izzy paid for Hank to go to college at Leigh University and gave him a job in his factory. He also paid for Hank to go to summer camp and gave him a $1,000 when he got married. Izzy loved Hank and treated him as one of his sons. Sylvia and Edith Weinstein were both born in Brooklyn. After a few years, Izzy bought an existing shirt factory in Northampton, Pennsylvania, which already had the name, Clyde Shirt, and the family moved to Allentown, Pennsylvania in 1932.

Between the arrival of Zvi Hirsh and Esther in 1922 and through the death of Rabbi Zvi Hirsch Paretzky in 1933, the family has centered itself around their home. Every Sunday, all the children and grandchildren would come to visit them for tea. Ruth Poretzky Hershkovitz remembers that Tzvi Hirsch taught her the Yiddish alphabet while sitting on his lap. Later, she would send him postcards and he would send them back corrected. Ruth remembers Hirsch and Esther as very kind and loving people.

Tzvi Hirsch and Esther Sarah ran a very Orthodox home. Ruth Paretzky Hershkovitz remembers that when the family would go visit them on holidays or Sabbaths, they would have to arrive before the Sabbath or Yomtov began. She remembers that Tzvi Hirsch would come home from shul, wash up, and call all the children and grandchildren into the dining room where he would place his hands on their heads and bless them in Hebrew, "May you be like Sarah, Rebecca, Rachel, and Leah. May the Lord bless you and protect you. May the Lord smile on you and be gracious to you. May the Lord show you favor and give you peace." On many instances, specifically during holidays, the men would sit at one table with the boys, and the women and girls would sit at another table. During Sukkot, the other women would sit inside the home, not outside in the Sukkah.

Breina Bertha Paretzky. Location and date unknown.

On *Pesech*, the *sedarim* would last a long time since all the children had to ask the four questions, find the *afikoman*, and Zvi Hirsch had to bless all the children. Ruth Paretzky Hershkovitz remembers that Esther would bring all the grandchildren into the kitchen and give them food to eat so they could stay up for the long night of the *seder*. Sylvia Weinstein remembers that Esther would travel to Allentown and take care of the children and make them food and study Jewish texts all day. Ruth Paretzky Hershkovitz remembers Esther as a tall woman, about the same height as Rabbi Hirsch. Esther was about equal height to her husband and had the presence of a matriarch. She was broadly built and controlled the house and had a great presence within it. Rabbi Zvi Hirsch didn't speak English and neither did Esther. Ruth Paretzky Hershkovitz remembers Esther as someone driven by a sense of duty. This was different from Basha Poretzkyn Epstein, Rabbi Zvi Hirsch's sister, who was an exceptionally warm and affectionate person and who told Ruth Paretzky Hershkovitz stories in Yiddish. Sylvia Weinstein remembers Esther Sarah sitting on the front porch, alone, reading her prayers.

Rabbi Tzvi Hirsch Paretzky. Date and location unknown.

It was in this warm, loving, and supportive context that an entire extended Paretzky family, three generations, all living near one another in Brooklyn, raised a whole new generation of American Paretzkys, Powers, and Porets. Parents and children were close to one another and respected one another. Torah, Jewish, and social justice values were discussed often. Grandchildren developed personal relationships with their grandparents and saw them on a weekly or bi-weekly basis.

Cousins, close and distant, played with one another, supported one another, did business together, gave one another loans, got and gave each other jobs, built one another up professionally and personally, attended school together, socialized together, and generally looked after one another irrespective of education or economic status.

Esther Sarah Dubrow with her granddaughter, Ruth Poretzky. Circa 1936.

An example of this can be found between the Paretzky-Shulman sisters and the Paretzky-Rutstein children. According to Ethel Shulman (the daughter of Haddie Poretzky and granddaughter of Mordechai Paretzky), one-time Bessie Poretsky Rutstein got sick with an ulcer, and because Haddie was a nurse, she went to take care of Bessie. When Ethel got married, Bessie Poretzky Rutstein sent her a beautiful tablecloth and assisted Haddie in numerous other ways, including financially. The two took care of one another. Ethel remembers that Bessie's daughter, Rita Rutstein, would call her all the time when she was a student at Cornell because she missed her. Ethel remembers that Milton Rothstein, Rita's brother, and Ethel's sister, Bella, were both in touch with each other regularly because both Milton and Bella liked music (Bella was a music major). The two corresponded extensively on the subject. There are countless examples of these types of relationships between cousins. Most of these types of relationships would last through the 1950s, and some for a little bit longer.

Rabbi Zvi Hirsch died on January 2, 1933 and was buried in Montefiore Cemetery. Esther Sarah Poretzky died in 1942. After the funeral of Esther Sarah, the children found a *kittel*, in which Jews are traditionally buried, which Esther had sewn by hand and hid under her pillow.

Left photograph: Esther Sarah Dubrow at the tombstone of her husband Hirsch. Circa 1933. Right photograph: Leah Paretzky Brickman and Shea Paretzky Plotkin with her son Hank Plotkin at Esther's gravesite, circa 1942. Brooklyn, New York.

Unfortunately, Esther had been buried in another *kittel,* but the children were distraught that they didn't know that she had prepared her own in anticipation of death, made according to the specifications of Jewish law.

In the years after that the death of the Paretzky patriarch and matriarch, the family both assimilated and acculturated into American Society. They changed their names to Poret, Powers, Paretsky, Poretsky. They migrated from Brooklyn, New York to New Jersey, to Los Angeles, California, and

43

everywhere in between. Many Paretzkys became successful doctors, lawyers, accountants, engineers, and businesspeople. Some became multi-millionaires many times over. The descendants of Moshe Bunim Poretzky contributed to American society, most maintained their Jewish identities, were productive citizens, but never forgot where they came from.

1923 Poretzky Family Portrait. Top row, from left to right: Nathan Paretzky, Goldie Okul, Leah Paretzky, Sadie Tziporah Epstein Poretzky, Harry Paretzky, Tziporah Celia Paretzky. Second Row, from left to right: Bertha Paretzky, Betty Poratzky, Frank Poret, Yvette (Yetta?) Poret, Sylvia Poret. Third row down: Max Paretzky, Annie, Tzvi Hirsch Paretzky, Esther Sarah Dubrow, Jacob Poret, Anna (her section of the picture deteriorated). Bottom row: Murray Poretzky (son of Nathan and Goldie), Sidney Poretzky (son of Max and Anna); Murray Poret (son of Jacob and Anna); Ruth Paretzky (daughter of Harry and Sadie); Rhoda Paretzky and Sylvia Paretzky (daughters of Nathan and Golda).

APPENDIX

Other Biographical Details About the Children of Zvi Hirsch and Esther Paretzky

1. MAX MORDECHAI SHMUEL PORETSKY was born in 1881 in Tolochin, Belarus. He was the oldest of the boys. He died on August 23, 1935 in Brooklyn, New York, of a heart attack. He married Anna Cheifetz in New York. She was born in 1888, probably in Tolochin, Belarus. She died in 1953 in Brooklyn, New York. Max was a happy, jovial person and liked to drink and play cards. He did well in the construction business but eventually lost most of it during the great depression.

    Max and Anna had four children. They were: (1) Isidor Poretsky born in 1908. He died in 1944; (2) Betty Poretsky was born in 1909 in Brooklyn, New York. She died in 2001 in Florida. She married Merrill Jacobs in 1928 in Brooklyn, New York. He was born in 1907 in Brooklyn, New York. He died in March 1973 in Florida; (3) Yetta Poretsky was born in 1911 in Brooklyn, New York. She died in 1985 in Florida. She married Mendel Bauman in 1930 in Brooklyn, New York. He was born in 1909 in Chanawith, Austria. He died in 1995 in

    Max Poretzky and his son Sidney. New York, circa 1924.

    Florida; (4) Sidney Poret was born in 1920 in Brooklyn, New York. He married Charlotte Koller in 1948 in Philadelphia, Pennsylvania. She was born in 1916 in Philadelphia. She died in 1990 in Florida.

2. JACOB YAAKOV PORET was born in 1887 in Tolochin, Mogilev Gurburnia, Belarus. He died in 1964 in Brooklyn, New York. He married Anne Nemrowsky in 1910. She was born in 1891 in the United States. She died in 1950 in Brooklyn, New York. Jacob and Anna had four children. They were: (1) Frances Poret born in 1912. He died in 1980 in Brooklyn, New York. He married Pearl Salzman in 1941 in New York, New York. She was born in 1920. She died in 1990 in Leverett, Massachusetts; (2) Sylvia Poret born in Brooklyn, New York. She died in 1982 in New Jersey. She married Irvin Weber on 20 Apr 1940 in New York, at the Plaza Hotel. He was born in 1912 in New York City. He died in 2000 in Connecticut; (3) Murray Poret was born in 1919 in Brooklyn, New York. He died in 1979 in Brooklyn, New York. He married Fay Berman in 1945 in New York, New York. She was born in 1912 in New York; (4) Aaron Poret was born in 1931 in Brooklyn, New York. He died in 1997 in Scottsdale, Arizona. He married Barbara Lieberman in 1956 in New York, New York. She was born in 1936 in Brooklyn, New York.

Jacob, Anna and Frank Poret. New York, Circa 1914.

According to Charles and Barry Poret, Jacob's first US job was as a bricklayer. Later he became a builder. He moved to Brooklyn and lived in a building that he built. His grandchildren still live there. Jacob also built a synagogue on Ocean Parkway called Ocean Parkway Jewish Center. Jacob was written about in a book about builders in Brooklyn. According to Barry Poret:

"The oral tradition, as I have heard it so many times, is that Jacob Poretsky, whose dad I believe but perhaps his granddad was a Rabbi, came to Ellis Island in 1906, with "ten-dollar equivalent in his pocket." The name was shortened to Poret at Ellis Island. Jacob ostensibly came from a small town around Kiev[24] during the pogroms in 1906. After Jacob came here, he ultimately brought over his siblings. Jacob was a bricklayer. He the built private homes, then three four-story walkups, then his crown jewel and the only remaining property, a 140-apartment building in Bayridge, Brooklyn, one of the most beautiful buildings in the city, named by my dad, his eldest son, The Colonnades.

Jacob's four children lived there after their marriages, and I was born and raised there. Jacob was written up in Who is Who of American Builders."

3. BASHA BESSIE PORETZKY was born in March 1888 in Tolochin, Mogilev Guberniya, Belarus. She died in February 1957 in Brooklyn, New York. She married Jacob Rutstein, son of Dov Ber Rutshtein and Rivka Shpitzgloz. Jacob was born on April 15, 1878 in Tolochin, Mogilev Guberniya, Belarus. Jacob died on February 27, 1946 in Brooklyn, New York.

The couple had five children: (1) Bertha Rutstein was born in 1909 in New York. She died in 1999 in Florida. She married Abraham Becker. He was born in 1907. He died in May 1986 in Albany, NY; (2) Dora Rothstein was born in 1910 in New York City, New York. She died in 1995. She married Joseph Bloom; (3) Nathan Rothstein was born in 1911 in Brooklyn, New York. He died in 1994 in Florida. He married Helen Jacobs on September 14, 1941 at the Brooklyn

---

[24] He must mean Minsk.

Jewish Center. She was born in 1918 in Brooklyn, New York. She died in April 1995 in Florida; (4) Morris Milton Rothstein was born on July 28, 1916 in Brooklyn, New York. He died on June 11, 1999 in Reno, Nevada. He married Bernice Bronster, daughter of Henry Bronsther and Hannah Gross on September 2, 1945 in Brooklyn, New York. She was born on August 7, 1922 in Brooklyn, New York; (5) Rita Rutstein was born December 10, 1928 in New York City, New York. She married Gerald Kaplan. He was born on December 19, 1927 in New York.

4. AARON HARRY PARETZKY was born in Feb 1890 in Tolochin, Mogiliv Gurburnia, Belarus. He died in 1972 in Brooklyn. New York. He married Sadie Tziporah Epstein. She was born on December 23, 1892 in Orsha, unter nerbia, Mogilev Gurburnia, Belarus. She died in 1988 in Florida. According to Ruth Paretzky Hershkovitz, her parents sent her to school at the Workman's Circle. Later in life, Harry became a socialist and was very politically liberal. The couple had two children: Ruth Paretzky Hershkovitz was born in 1921 in Brooklyn, New York. She married Emmanuel Hershkovitz in 1943 in Brooklyn, New York. He was born in New York, and Betty Paretzky was born in 1927 in Brooklyn, New York. She married David Grutman in 1951 in Brooklyn, New York. He was born in 1922 in Brooklyn, New York. He died in 2000 in Florida.

Harry, Sadie, Ruth and Betty Paretzky. New York. Circa 1927.

5. NATHAN NACHUM PORETZKY was born in 1894 in Tolochin, Belarus. He died in 1948 in Brooklyn, New York. He married Goldie

Okul. She was born in 1895 in Warsaw, Poland. She died in 1962 in Florida, United States. Nathan Poretzky and Goldie Okul had the following children: (1) Maurice Powers was born in Brooklyn, New York. He died in 1996 in Oakland, California. He married Leah Finkelstein. She was born in Brooklyn, New York; (2) Rhoda Paretzky was born in 1915 in Brooklyn, New York. She died in 1959. She married Frank Field in 1941 in Brooklyn, New York. He was born in 1915 in New York. He died in 1995 in New York City, United States; (3) Sylvia Paretzky was born in 1918 in Brooklyn, New York. She died in 2002 in Florida. She married Morris Brody in 1948 in Brooklyn, New York. He was born in 1907 in Brooklyn, New York. He died in 1984 in Blountstown, Florida.

Golda had arrived from Europe at the age of sixteen and was living with her aunt Anna, Max's Paretzky's wife, and that is how the couple met. According to Harmon Brody, "Nathan married Golda; had five children, of which three survived. Nathan worked as a baker and union organizer and helped found the New York baker's union." Nathan would eventually go into the wrecking business and construction until the Second World War.

Harmon Brody writes:

"Nathan was a lifelong democrat. He was a national committeeman and Union organizer. His profession had been as a cake baker, and he helped to start the cake baker's union in the sweatshops of the bakeries in New York. He took many beatings at the hands of the shop owners. He was dedicated to the working class, to the little guy, who had no one to protect him, to the poor man who needed help.

Nathan gave to charity and donated many hours to helping the poor. He had been a religious and an Orthodox Jew but abandoned (giving time to) that part of his life, instead of giving his time to the labor movement. When World War Two came, he was a very patriotic citizen, but too old to serve. He had many political connections through the unions and also through the synagogues. Maurice, Nathan's son, and Nathaniel's father also were very politically motivated as was my mother by Nathan. They were quite liberally minded. They sought to get educated and expand their minds and learn as much as they could and contribute to society.

Maurice became a professor through Colombia and an artist while my mother went to Brooklyn College and worked as a legal secretary to the New York Prosecutor at the time. Because she was a woman, she wasn't taken as seriously as a man in her day and that was something that bothered her…

The Family of Nathan Paretzky. New York, circa 1940s.

What I know about the rest of the family and politics is what my mother told me. That we have always stood for those who need the strength of others. That it is our duty to be there for those who cannot be there for themselves--to help them be strong and complete. That our work is never done. That relieving suffering is the greatest mitzvah..."

6. BERTHA PORETZKY was born on January 2, 1900 in Tolochin, Mogilev Gurburnia, Belarus. She died on May 23, 1983 in Allentown, Pennsylvania. She married Isidor Weinstein, son of Loppel Lieb Weinstein and Yetta, in March 1927 in Brooklyn. He was born in Littin Podyner, Russia. He died on April 21, 1968 in Allentown, Pennsylvania. Bertha was said to be the prettiest of the sisters. Izzy chased Bertha and was very in love with her. They had three children together: (1) Sylvia Weinstein born in 1928 in New York, New York. She married Ben Ami Sussman in 1948 at the Brooklyn Jewish Center. He was born in 1925 in Philadelphia, Pennsylvania; (2) Edith Weinstein was born on May 17, 1931 in Brooklyn, New York. She married Chester Miller in 1950 in Forest Hills, New York. He was born in 1929 in Brooklyn, New York; (3) Harris Weinstein was born in 1935 in Allentown, Pennsylvania. He married (a) Debbie Plarr in 1976 and (b) Sandra Levy in 1957 in New York.

7. SHEA CELIA PORETZKY was born in 1902 in Tolochin, Belarus. She died in Brooklyn, New York in the United States. Shea took care of her parents during their last years. She married Benjamin Plotkin when she was in her thirties. He was born in 1890 and died in 1973. Shea was very different from her sisters and described as a free spirit and a "character."

Benjamin had been married before but divorced his first wife to marry Shea. The couple had one son, Harris or Hank Plotkin. Harris Plotkin was born in 1935 in Brooklyn, New York. He married Ruth Wedeen on August 24, 1958 in Newark, New Jersey. She was born in 1938 in Perth Amboy, New Jersey.

According to Hank Plotkin, when Shea was pregnant, she had a dream of two lights going in other directions. So, she named him Harris Max Plotkin for the two names, from two different lights (i.e. from both families). Shea had many boyfriends in her youth, but she was not allowed to marry until her older sister got married. After Bertha and Izzy married, Shea married Ben Plotkin. Ben had been "The Flying Tailor" for the Navy in California before he married Shea. Shea and Ben honeymooned in the Catskills. They then stayed on and ran a bar and grille in the Catskills called "Shea's Bar and Grille." After their son was born, "Shea decided she didn't want her baby crawling on the floor among the drunks, so they left the bar and the Catskills. Uncle Jake Poret offered them an apartment in his building at 3030 Brighton 12th Street if Ben would become the house painter. Bubbie Esther, Leah, Shea, Ben, and Harris all lived together in that apartment. The years of painting took their toll and Ben developed lung problems. At that point, they moved to Allentown and Izzy Weinstein set them up in a retail clothing business."

Shea Poretzky, date and location unknown.

8. LEAH LILLIAN PARETZKY was born in 1905 in Oriol, Tolochin, Belarus. Leah was the youngest. She married three times. She married a very handsome man named Milton. The marriage lasted a very short time and was either annulled or ended in divorce. Leah married another time "but the marriage was annulled because he was a fairy." According to Ruth Paretzky Hershkovitz, in one of her marriages, her husband disappeared. Rumor had it he had wanted to return to Europe to take care of his sick mother but that Leah, who had experienced persecution, refused to return to Europe under any circumstances. Leah was devastated at being abandoned and had a broken heart. The exact details of the story were never related. After that negative experience, Leah married a taxi driver she met in New York, Max Brickman. They had a stillborn baby. Leah and Max came to Allentown and lived in the Weinstein attic for a short time until Izzy Weinstein set them up in a small haberdasher shop in Philadelphia. She had no children.

Leah Paretzky. Date and location unknown.

Photographs of Unknown Paretzky Family Members

Below are photographs of unidentified Paretzky family members, taken in Europe. These may be photos of the siblings murdered in the pogroms, or photos taken of the surviving siblings in Europe, or a combination of both.

Acknowledgments

This history would not be possible without the research and testimony of Ruth Paretzky Hershkovitz, Bonnie Brodie, Hank Plotkin, Sylvia Weinstein, Edith Weinstein, Beth Levy, Rana Morris, Rebecca Grutman, and others. This history synthesizes their research into a single narrative about the first generations of the Poretzkyn family in America[25].

---

[25] This history also attempts to answer the questions asked by Bonnie Brodie in 1988, where she asked: What is the name of the village that Esther came from? What were the names of the brothers and sisters who didn't make it? Was Harris (Hirsch) the Rabbi, wise man or cantor of the village? Did he also do something else to make a living? Did everyone come to the U.S. together? Did Jacob come first and then send to everyone else?

PART III

THE NACHUM RUTSTEIN FAMILY OF TOLOCHIN, BELARUS

Nachum Rutstein[26] was likely born in greater Tolochin, then part of White Russia, a region of the Russian Empire, in the second or third decade of the 19th century (1820s or 1830s). Nachum Rutstein's tribe appears to have been concentrated in the region between the city of Minsk and the town of Orsha. That Rutstein tribe settled in smaller hamlets or villages, primarily Tolochin and a smaller hamlet nearby, Kochanova, which is between the towns of Orsha and Tolochin[27].

---

[26] The origin of the surname Rothstein: the following is taken from the Beth Hatefutsoth Encyclopedia of Jewish Names. It provides different theories as to the origin of the surname which in German means Redstone:

Many Jews bear names based on places of origin or residence. Rotstein is a toponymic surname (i.e. derived from a place of origin or residence), associated with the town of Rot near Nuremberg in Bavaria. Stein is a common suffix of Jewish family names. It could be toponymic too. All localities called Stein (the German for "stone" and/or "Rock") are situated near Nuremberg, Bavaria, Krems, Niederosterreich (Austria), and Schaffhaused (Switzerland). Kamnik in Slovenia is still in German, and the name of a number of places in Poland called Kamien has been translated by Jews into the Yiddish Shteyn. Rot was also often a nickname for a man with red hair or beard, which became part of the family name.

In the 20th century, Rotstajn [and its related variations of the spelling of the surnames] are recorded as a Jewish family surname.

[27] Members of the Tolochin Rutstein family have spelled the surname as follows: Rothstein, Rutstein, Rotstein, Rootshtein, Rotchstein, and Rutshtein and many other variants. The author is of the opinion that most Rothsteins (the variety of spelling is of no genealogical significance) are not related to this family. The author, however, has come across a number of Rothsteins in his research from the province of Minsk, who are seemingly related. This is especially true of those Rothsteins that originate from the vicinity of Orsha and Tolochin. Looking at many records in the archives, seeing the repetition of family names, it became clear that there was an unknown Rothstein progenitor, perhaps the father or grandfather of Nachum Rutstein, who initially adopted the surname, and which over time produced many different branches of the family throughout the greater Tolochin area. The Rothstein men of this family are Israelites and are members of Y-Chromosome Haplotype G2a2.

Nachum was born into a world where Jews were treated as second class citizens and state sponsored antisemitism, persecution and pogroms of Jews were the norm. This physical, economic, legal, and social persecution created great societal dysfunction and provided numerous obstacles to the advancement of Jews trying to eke out a living. Through sheer tenacity, however, Nachum became a wealthy, resourceful, and established businessman—possibly making his fortune in the lumber and real estate industries. Nachum owned real estate throughout Tolochin and possibly in the nearby hamlet of Kochanova. Nachum was a proud Jew, and he used his wealth to support Jewish life and peoplehood. Archival research reveals that Nachum Rutstein was the father of at least three children (but likely many more). The name of his three known sons are Ephraim, Shimon[28], and Dov Behr[29].

It was perhaps Nachum Rutstein who was the protagonist of a story told by Gregg Rothstein regarding another 'Rothstein' family of Tolochin. There was once a certain Yitzchak "Itsko" Soloveitchik (1818 – Est. 1900), who hailed from a long rabbinic line, whose roots were in the Igumun province in modern-day Belarus, and who had migrated to Tolochin with his three sons. The legend relates that two of his young sons, Avraham and Yisroel Dov Ber, were drafted into the Russian army. Russian law at the time provided that should a family have only one son, that son would be exempt from the Russian army. A common means of evading military service was to send the "extra" son to another family who either had no other son or was in another way able to shelter the child. The two Soloveitchik sons went to live with two other Tolochin families, one of them with the surname Berger, and the other Rothstein. Because Yisrael Dov Ber was assisted in some way by the

---

[28] Shimon Rutstein was born in the Mogliev region of Belarus. His existence is known only through archival records which provide the following information: "The following is a list of the cases to be heard by Mogilev Guberniya Criminal Court on the 12th of December, 1879…5. Re. meshanin Simon Nokhimov Rutstein accused of a thievery."

[29] That Ephraim and Dov Behr were brothers can also be inferred from the passenger manifests of the ship Graf Waldersee in which provide that their children Leizer Rutstein and Basya Rutstein respectively are listed as having traveled together to America and arriving on September 25, 1908. In the ship manifest, Ephraim and Behr respectively are listed as their fathers. The record provides that Basya had previously immigrated to the United States but Leizer had not.

Nachum Rutstein family of Tolochin, Yisrael Dov Ber changed his surname from Soloveitchik to Rodstein in honor of the family of Nachum Rutstein. Itsko's descendants still carry the surname Rothstein, (and its spelling variants) until today[30]. The author posits, based on his review of the archival records, that to distinguish themselves, the families spelled the name differently. The family of Nachum Rutstein spelled Rutstein in Russian as **Рутштейн** and the family of Yisroel Dov Behr Rothstein as **Рудштейн**.

Despite Nachum's great success and great kindness to others, at least two of his children succumbed to the social ills which surrounded them. According to Milton Rothstein, "Dov Behr's two oldest brothers gambled their father's fortune and business away--mostly in card games[31]." Dov Behr, however, it appears, refrained from the reckless gambling practices of his older brothers. Attempting to retain what he could of the legacy and fortune of Nachum Rutstein, Dov Behr remained conservative in his business and personal affairs. He is not known to have gambled. Nor does it appear that he took any great risk in business. He did, however, manage to eke out a simple living and provide support to his ten children.

Ephraim Rutstein was born in Tolochin, Belarus, the son of Nachum Rutstein. He married Sivia "Tzivia" Porchevnik the daughter of Avraham Porchevnik. The couple had at least six children. A 1904 notice in the Mogilevskie Gubernskie Vedomosti, a local newspaper, provides that the Moscow Sted (Agrarian Land) Bank announced that the "below real estate belonging to the persons who didn't return the loans to the bank will be sold at auction at November 18, 1904." Among the names are "Ephraim Nukhimovich Rutshtein, 1st district of the town, Mogilevskaya street, land area 203 sq. 'sazhen' [about 925 sq. m.], unpaid debt 1278 rubles 30 kopeeks" which at this time was about. US $650[32]. A 1911 notice in the same newspaper

---

[30] Y-chromosome DNA results conducted on one male descendant of Yisrael Dov Ber Solevitchik provide inconclusive answers as to whether there was a distant paternal family relationship to Nachum Rutstein. The families were likely related in some manner, perhaps maternally.

[31] The names of the older brothers are not known.

[32] These debts may be a result of fines and sanctions imposed on the family as a result of its sons' failure to appear for the military draft.

provides that the Orsha *uezd* (province) police department was searching for Leizer Nokhim, the son of Ephraim Rutstein, and his family due to his failure to appear in 1910 for a military draft. The notice states that the police were specifically looking for: (i) father, Ephraim Rutstein the son of Nachum Rutstein, (ii) mother, Tziviya the daughter of Avraham; and brothers (iii) Girsha; (iv) Simon Nota; and (v) his sister Genesha." Oral history relates that two of Nachum's grandchildren married one another. Dov Behr's son Nisson Rutstein, married Frayda Rutstein, the daughter of Ephraim Rutstein. Oral history provides no other details regarding Ephraim[33].

A possible photo of Ephraim Rutstein. Courtesy of Inna Sorin. Tolochin, Belarus. Date unknown.

---

[33] There is a fifty-percent chance the photo on the right is that of Ephraim Rutstein or one of Ephraim's other siblings or Rutstein cousins.

The Life of Dov Behr "Berka" Rutstein

Dov Behr Rutstein (Est. 1845 – Est. 1913), who was called Behr or Berka, is believed to have been born in greater Tolochin, Belarus, in the fourth or fifth decade of the 1800s into a wealthy family that was a supporter and patron of Jewish life. Milton Rothstein reports that "Dov Behr's father" Nachum "was reported to have been a very wealthy man" and used that wealth to help others. However, Behr's older brothers gambled and squandered Nachum's fortune leaving Behr with significantly reduced assets or in poverty.

Archival research reveals that in 1874 or 1875, Behr, still a young man, was drafted into the Russian Army. This event would have been traumatic to Nachum who lived through the age of the Cantonist schools, *khappers* (kidnappers), and other discriminatory policies of Czar Nicholas I. From 1827 to 1874, Nachum and his wife had witnessed children as young as eight years old drafted into the Russian Army for twenty-five-year terms where many of these children suffered from starvation, physical and psychological pressure to convert to Christianity[34]. It was not unusual for a twelve-year-old boy to be drafted, to serve twenty-five years, and then come out of the army at the age of 37 only to begin his life. Few of the children drafted into the Russian army were able to remain observant Jews during military service, and the majority of those that survived did not ever see their families again. The military draft devastated the Jewish community, increased class tensions, and eroded confidence in rabbinic leadership. It created a consistent sense of panic among Jewish parents, including Nachum, that their children could be taken away from them by the state.

However, lucky for Behr, in 1874, Alexander II engaged in a series of reforms that reduced military service to six years and raised the draft age to 21 (although in reality, children much younger were still drafted). It is unclear whether Behr actually served full time in the military or was, alternatively, as

---

[34] See Yohanan Petrovsky-Shtern, Jews in the Russian Army, 1827-1917: Drafted into Modernity. Cambridge and New York, Cambridge University Press, 2009.

a landowner and the child of a wealthy man, able to purchase his release from the military. His military service must not have been that extensive service, or he must have been a member of the reserves because Behr's first known child was born in 1876.

Milton Rothstein, grandson of Dov Behr, relates that Behr was a giant of a man who was over 6'4 and weighed 260 pounds and had powerful muscles. Behr was reputed to be the strongest man in his *gurbernia* or state. Behr is reputed to have picked up a full-grown horse, perhaps as heavy as 1500 pounds. According to Steven Rothstein, Behr picked up a horse by going underneath the horse with his body and using his shoulders to pick up the horse while using his legs as a support. According to Jay Rothstein, the horse may have been picked up in the context of a dare or competition.

Dov Behr was considered a local hero and was called a *"gibbur"* in Yiddish/Hebrew. According to Milton Rothstein, during and after pogroms, Dov Behr organized local Jews and formed Jewish defense organizations. Individually and together, these heroes or *"gibburim,"* would defend Jewish women, children, and property against assault and pillaging. After the pogroms, the *gibburim* would retaliate against the Cossacks that had murdered, slaughtered, and massacred their friends, family, and other defenseless Jews in cold blood. It was reported that in at least one instance Dov Behr strangled one of these Cossacks with his bare hands. After the Cossacks would attack, raid, rape, and pillage, the Cossacks would go to the local saloon to get drunk and celebrate and boast about their killing of Jews. In at least one or more instances, Behr waited for the guilty and drunk Cossack to come out of the saloon, and whether there was one or two of them, Behr would come up behind them and strangle them to death with his bare hands. It is likely that these events took place between 1881 and 1884 when a series of pogroms swept the Pale of Settlement following the assassination of Alexander II.

Dov Behr was married at least twice. According to Alan Redstone, Dov Behr's first wife[35] died in Belarus. Her name is unknown. Dov Behr then remarried to Riva Rothstein. Riva was the daughter of Yisrael Rothstein and Frieda Pavcek and was a cousin[36]. Riva was born on April 1, 1847, likely in

---

[35] According to Boris Rutstein, Dov Ber Rutstein had Ely Rutstein as a child with his first wife:

i.   Ely Rutstein. Years ago, after my visit to Tolochin, I met Rutshtein cousins in Israel who connected with this family (although I cannot tell you exactly how). According to memory, Michael Rutshtein of Ashdod related that Dov Behr is reported to have had a child named Ely Rutstein with his first wife and who also stayed behind in Belarus. Ely Rutshtein had the following children: (i) Nachum Rutshtein who married Tzirah; and (ii) Mina Rutshtein. I found Nachum's Ruthstein's tombstone in Tolochin. Nachum Rutshtein and Tzirah had the following children: (i) Boris Ruthstein; (2) Ely Ruthstein (who has daughters who live in Noginsk near Moscow and who was an engineer; (iii) Michael Rutshtein. I met Boris Rutshtein as an old man in Ashdod, Israel, and he remembered his uncle Yaakov Rutstein visiting Tolochin in the 1930s. Boris Rutshtein had the following children: (i) Michael Rutshtein; (ii) Sonya Rutshtein Krivoshey, who has sons named Dani and Alex. Michael Rutshtein (son of Nachum Ruthstein) had Dina Rutshtein Vili and has four children one of whom is named Tali. Michael Rutshtein (son of Boris Ruthstein) has the following children: (i) Rami Rutshtein; and (ii) Natan Ruthstein, both of Ashdod, Israel.

(Nachum, his wife, and their child, Boris)

[36] Archival research reveals an 1884 reference to an Israel Ber Rothstein in the Mogilevskie Gubernskie Vedomosti, a local newspaper. Although it's possibly a reference to Riva's parents or another member of our Rothstein family, it is more likely a reference to the family of Isaac Solevitchik whose son Yisrael Ber adopted the surname Rothstein. The newspaper account provides:

The fire which took place on the 10th of March destroyed the Jewish community *mikva* and five private houses with belongings. The owners of the houses were local Jews: Israel Berka Rodshtein, Leiba Zusin, Chaya-Ryvka Khotovkin, Abram Alkins, and David Alkins. The investigation showed that on the night of March 9 a local peasant Ivan Shopik was using the stove to make the *mikva* warm and fell asleep. The fire began and destroyed all the neighboring houses belonging to the above-named

Tolochin. Riva married a man whose surname was Shpitzglas and then afterward married Dov Behr. Dov Behr and Riva were probably (first) cousins but this cannot be confirmed.

Dov Behr had at least ten children. According to Phyllis Birnbaum, when Rutstein children misbehaved, as a punishment, Riva or Behr sent them to go outside and fetch water from the well and river. The children did so, living with the fear that they could be kidnapped by Cossacks. Frayda, Dov

---

persons. The fire has damaged Staro-Tolochin Jewish Community for 2000 rubles, Rodshtein for 1000 rubles, Zusin for 300 rubles, Khotovkin for 150 rubles, Abram Alkin for 650 rubles, Dovid Alkin for 50 rubles, and Ryzh for 100 rubles.

In 1895, Israel Ber Rodshtein was elected and approved by the Mogilev Governor for a "Scholar Jew" position in Staro-Tolochin Great Synagogue, for three years (1895-1898). In 1896 or 1899, the family of Izrail-Berka Rodshtein was fined a penalty of 300 rubles for the non-appearance of its members for the military draft. The records also provide that Israel Berka died between 1896 and 1899. His heirs — widow Doba Simonova (the daughter of Simon) and children Nachum, Simkha-Chaim, and Sora Rodshtein — didn't pay the penalty. As a consequence, the state took their real estate (two or more properties) in Staro-Tolochin, and in Zarechno-Tolochinskaya street, and sold them.

On July 20th, 1910, the ship Birma arrived at Ellis Island. It contained passengers Dobe Radstein, widowed and then aged 70 years old, her son Nachum Radstein, then age 40, and Nachum's wife, Leie. Although it cannot be confirmed, it is believed that this Rutstein family belonged to the descendants of Itsko Solevitchik. This needs further confirmation.

(Yisrael Ber Rodshtein)

Behr's daughter, recalls fetching water as a child and being afraid that Cossacks would kidnap her.

Oral history provides that Dov Ber was a very poor man. However, 1906 land records provide that Berka Rutstein, the son of Nachum Rutstein, did own real estate in Staro-Tolochin and managed to provide for himself.

The last years of Behr's life parallel that of the decline of Jewish Tolochin and the emigration of its Jewish population. Two of Behr's children, Yisroel and Nisson, immigrated to the United States in 1911 to join their brother, Yaakov, in the new world. Behr, however, resisted emigration. In 1912, records provide that "Berka Rutstein" owned land in Tolochin and had a business in Kochanova. In 1912, Frada Rutstein, daughter of Ephraim Rutstein, lists her Uncle "Behr" as a point of contact in Europe on her immigration form. The document provides that Behr was then living in Kochanova 12 miles east of Tolochin.

On October 27th, 1913, Riva immigrated to the United States and went to live with her son Yaakov at 65-67 Kings Street in Brooklyn, New York. In New York, Riva lived for a few short years and helped take care of her grandchildren, including bathing Bessie Boyarin, her granddaughter, as a child.

Riva died on July 25, 1921 in Brooklyn, New York, and is buried in Queens, New York. According to Jay Rothstein, Dov Behr also immigrated to the United States. However, no documentary evidence has been located that confirms that assertion. According to Jay Rothstein, Behr died in a Turkish bathhouse in the United States. Behr reportedly drank cold water and it was believed that the sudden change in temperature sent his body into shock and killed him. The author, however, believes that Behr died in Kochanova, Belarus in or around late 1912 or early 1913 – in the Turkish or public bathhouse as described in the story of Jay Rothstein. The author based this on the fact that Riva presumably emigrated after his death. A grandson of Behr, Bernard Rutstein, was born in 1914 and was named after him. With the death of Behr in 1914, the history of the centuries long presence of the Rutstein family in Tolochin comes to a close.

Rivka "Riva" Rothstein-Rutstein and Dov Behr Rutstein. Tolochin, Belarus. Est. 1911.

APPENDIX

The Children of Ephraim Rutstein and Sivia Porchevnik

1. FRADIE RUTSTEIN was born on January 31, 1886 in Kochanova, Mogiliv Gubernia, Belarus. She immigrated to the United States on September 16, 1912. She died on December 28, 1967 in Brooklyn, New York. She married her first cousin, Nathan Rutstein.

2. SHIMON RUTSTEIN was born on January 1, 1887 in Tolochin, Belarus. He died on September 16, 1948 in Brooklyn, New York. He married Hanna Rosenthal on June 22, 1913 in Bronx, New York. She was born on February 16, 1892 in Bialystok, Belarus. She died on January 21, 1950 in Brooklyn, New York. Shimon and Hannah had the following children: (a) Bernard Rutstein was born on January 20, 1914 in Brooklyn, New York. He died on August 18, 1994 in Indiana. He married Sophie Axelrod on February 27, 1938 in New York. She was born on July 04, 1917 in Brooklyn, New York. She died on November 29, 1995 in Indiana; (b) Evelyn Rutstein was born on May 01, 1916 in Brooklyn, New York. She died on February 12, 1984 in Kendall Park, New Jersey. She married David Wexler on December 03, 1939 in Brooklyn, New York. He was born on November 14, 1910 in New York, New York. He died on February 04, 1969 in Manhattan, New York; (c)

Shimon and Hannah Rutstein.

Irving Rutstein was born on March 04, 1921 in Brooklyn, New York. He died on December 16, 1972 in Philadelphia, Pennsylvania. He married Ruth Sterenberg on April 09, 1942 in Brooklyn, New York. She was born on March 13, 1922 in Brooklyn, New York. Irving's son, Hanan Rutstein, made *aliyah*, became Orthodox, lives in Maalat Michmas, and has four children and many grandchildren.

Shimon Rutstein won $5,000 in a lottery while living in Buenos Aires. He courted his wife and were fairly well-to-do, owning a vehicle and having a maid.

3. GNESJA RUTSTEIN was born in 1888 in Tolochin, Mogiliv Gubernia, Belarus. She died on December 18, 1959 in Brooklyn, New York. She married Benyamin Hoffenberg. He was born in 1885 in Russia. He died on November 06, 1953 in Brooklyn, New York. Benyamin Hoffenberg and Gnesja Rutstein had the following children: (a) Nathan Hoffenberg was born on September 09, 1918 in Brooklyn, New York. He married Yetta Wurtzel on March 03, 1944 in Brooklyn, New York. She was born on January 10, 1925 in Manhattan, New York; (b) Abraham Hoffenberg was born on September 09, 1918 in Brooklyn, New York. He married Shirley Silver in Nov 1941 in Brooklyn, New York. She was born on June 22, 1920 in New York; (c) Samuel Hoffenberg was born after 1919. He died in 1985.

4. ELIEZER NACHUM "LAZER" RUTSTEIN was born on November 01, 1892 in Tolochin, Mogiliv Gubernia, Belarus. According to archival research, Lazer was drafted into the military in 1910 but did not report for duty. He died on December 18, 1977 in New York. He married Anna. Eliezer Rutstein and Anna had the following children: (a) Abraham Rutstein; (b) Gertrude Rutstein; (c) Hyman Rutstein; (d) Ida Helen Rutstein was born on December 05, 1917 in Brooklyn, New York. She died on April 05, 2002 in Florida. She married Harry Phillip Sperling in Brooklyn, New York. He was born on July 04, 1910 in Brooklyn, New York. He died in 1995 in Florida.

Archival research has revealed the following additional siblings who remained in Russia:

1. ISRAEL RUTSTEIN, who declared bankruptcy in Tolochin in 1910;

2. GIRSH RUTSTEIN OR HIRSCH RUTSTEIN (d. 1939). Hirsch, a carpenter by profession, married his cousin Genia Rutstein (d.1941). The couple remained behind in Tolochin (when his siblings and cousins went to America) and therefore became part of Soviet Jewry. Hirsch had at least four children: (1) Chaya (d.1941); (2) Chaim (d. 1945); (3) Zavel (1913 – 1986) (4) Golda (April 1916 - 2009). Chaya was sexually assaulted (and/or raped) in the pogroms before the Russian Revolution.

Zavel was a soldier in the Soviet Army and received many medals for bravery. He served in three wars: (1) Finland; (2) World War Two, where he served as an aviation technician and pilot and (3) Japan. He married Dora Rochlin (1921 – 1978), an orphan of the famines, and had three children, Georg (1942-1988), Valera (b.1947), and Slava (b.1951). Zavel was called to war the day after his wedding. He later reunited with his wife at the end of World War II.

Zavel and Chaim Rutstein. Smolensk, Soviet Union, 1934. Photo courtesy of Inna Rubina.

Genia (wife of Hirsch) and Chaya (along with her two children) were killed in 1941/1942 by the Nazi Einsatzgruppen. They are thought to be buried in a mass grave in or near Tolochin – possibly in the mass grave near the village of Raitsy with other Jewish Tolochiners. Chaim survived the Nazi Einsatzgruppen but disappeared at the end of, or immediately after, the Second World War.

Golda (Galina) grew up in a very poor family. Galina was the only child in her family to receive an education. Galina went to university and obtained a degree in teaching and Russian literature. Galina married Leibel Feldman (d. 1969) in 1937. She moved from Tolochin to Drybin where her husband had received a position as a prosecutor. The couple had their first child, Lilia, who died of a disease in 1939/1940. Golda then had a second child, Gregory (Girsch/Herschel), who was born 1939-40.

Golda Rutstein and Lev Feldman. Date and location unknown. Photo courtesy of Inna Rubina.

Sometime in the second half of 1941 and early 1942, Golda was in the vicinity of Drybin, and received news that her family and some of the other Jews that were in Tolochin had been murdered by the Nazis. At the same time, she received news that her husband's father had also been killed in or near Drybin. When she heard this news, Golda took her son Hirsh (who was then around two years old) and got on onto a train to travel east to a non-occupied zone of the Soviet Union. Golda looked very Jewish and the non-Jewish passengers, who were not used to seeing Jews, insulted and harassed her during the train ride. At some point during the journey, her son, Hirsh, became ill. Golda tried to conceal her son's illness but the people on the train discovered it. They were afraid that the child might be contagious. The non-Jewish passengers demanded that the conductor stop the train. They kicked Golda and Hirsh off the train. It was the middle of the winter. The train left them alone, in the middle of the forest, near a train station. Hirsh, Golda's son, died. Golda was forced to bury Hirsh, alone, with her own hands, in an isolated field.

Golda reunited with her husband in the non-occupied soviet zone near the city of Chkalov (Orenberg). In 1943, Golda gave birth to her daughter, Svetlana. After the war, Golda remained in Orenberg where she became a teacher. In 1950, she gave birth to another son, Gena Feldman. Gena drowned in summer camp at age 11 in 1961. In 1969, after the death of her husband, Golda moved to Moscow to help her daughter Svetlana (1943 – 1983) who had become ill. In 1996, as part of the wave of Soviet Jewish migration to the United States and Canada, Golda migrated to Montreal where she lived until her death in 2009 with her granddaughter and two great-grandchildren.

Golda Rutstein and her son Girsh Feldman (1940–1942). Drybin, Soviet Union, 1941.
Photo courtesy of Inna Rubina

The Children of Dov Ber Rutstein and Rivka "Riva" Rothstein-Shpitzgloz-Rutstein

1. FRAYDA RUTSTEIN was born on October 2, 1876 in Tolochin, Belarus. She died on September 24, 1924 in Brooklyn, New York. She married Max Mendel Boyarin in Tolochin, Belarus. He was born

in 1869 in Belarus. Max Mendel Boyarin and Frieda Rutstein had the following children: (i) Nathan Boyarer was born about 1902 in Tolochin, Belarus; (ii) Rose Boyarer was born about 1903 in Tolochin, Belarus; (iii) Meyer Boyarer was born about 1905 in Tolochin, Belarus; (iv) Bessie Boyarin was born on December 23, 1899 in Tolochin, Belarus. She died in October of 1985 in Rockaway, New Jersey. She married Ralph Markowitz. He was born about 1895 in Russia; (v) Elsie Boyarer Cohen, born in 1913 in New York.

2. MENDEL BOYARIN was not originally from Tolochin. Mendel was an apple merchant who sold apples wholesale. As an apple merchant, Mendel went from town to town unloading his wares. One day, as he was traveling, Mendel come to the Tolochin market to sell his apples. Mendel caught a glimpse of Frayda and fell instantly in love. Mendel was very tall, 6'4", broad-chested, good looking, and strong like Frayda's father, Dov Behr. The two married quickly.

According to Phyllis Birnbaum, Mendel had been drafted into the Russian army once in his youth and was drafted a second time as a young man. Mendel did not want to go into the Czarist army for a second time and so he left his wife and four kids in 1902 or 1903 so that he could go to the United States. Mendel only had enough money to get a ticket to England. He landed in England where he spent six months pressing pants and saving enough money to get to the United States, which he finally did. Mendel didn't write letters since he apparently was worried his location could be traced by the Russian government. In America, Yaakov Rutstein, Mendel's brother-in-law, sponsored Mendel's immigration and brought him into the lumber business with him. Mendel's experience also mirrors that of Yaakov Rutstein, in terms of emigrating to the US when faced with a second draft and staying in London for a time because of a lack of funds.

Once Mendel arrived in the United States, he sent for his wife and four kids. Yaakov Rutstein later also sponsored his sister, Frayda. Frayda felt safe immigrating to America because her brother, Jacob, had already paved the way for her and her husband.

Frayda and her children left Tolochin and traveled to the port on a wagon. During the journey, baby Nathan, then age two, fell off the wagon. Frayda and her children didn't notice that he had fallen off the wagon until they arrived at the port. They turned around and found him sleeping in the snow unaware of what had happened.

In America, Mendel went to go work in Yaakov Rutstein's lumber yard. Frayda Rutstein was a loving grandmother. She taught her grandson, Bert, how to speak Yiddish.

3. YAAKOV "YANKEL" RUTSTEIN was born on 15 Apr 1876/1877/1878 in Tolochin, Mogilev Guberniya, Belarus. He died on 27 February 1946 in Brooklyn, New York. He married Basha Poretzky, daughter of Rabbi Tzvi Hirsch Poretzkyn and Esther Sarah Dubrow in about 1907 in New York. She was born about 1885/1888 in Tolochin, Mogilev province, Belarus. She died in February 1957 in Brooklyn, New York, United States.

The couple had five children: (i) Bertha Rutstein was born on July 28, 1909 in Brooklyn, New York. She died on December 18, 1999 in Florida in the United States. She married Abraham Becker. He was born on April 17, 1907 in Albany, New York. He died on May 03, 1986 in Florida, United States.; (ii) Dora (Dvora) Rothstein was born in 1910 in New York, New York. She died about 1995. She married Dr. Joseph Bloom. They had two children: Dr. Harvey Bloom and Dr. Steven Bloom; (iii) Nathan (Nachum) Rothstein was born on April 13, 1911 in Brooklyn, New York. He died on January 28, 1994 in Boca Raton or Palm Beach, Florida. He married Helen Jacobs on September 14, 1941 in Brooklyn Jewish Center. She was born on June 16, 1918 in Brooklyn, New York. She died on April 08, 1995 in Florida; (iv) Morris Milton Rothstein was born on July 28, 1916 in Brooklyn, New York, United States. He died on June 11, 1999 in Reno, Nevada. He married Bernice Bronster, daughter of Henry Bronsther and Helen Hannah Gross on September 02, 1945 in Brooklyn, New York. She was born on August 07, 1922 in Brooklyn,

New York. She died on August 25, 2011 in Laguna Hills, Orange County, California; (v) Rita (Riva/Rivka) Rutstein was born on December 10, 1928 in New York City, New York. She married Gerald Frederick Kaplan. He was born on December 19, 1927 in New York, New York. More biographical details regarding Yaakov are referenced elsewhere.

4. GREGORY (GIRSH? OR HIRSCH) RUTSHTEIN was born between 1875-1880 in Kokhanavo, Mogiliv Gubernia, Belarus. His Hebrew name was lost due to Communism. Gregory died between 1916-1921 in Kokhanavo, Mogiliv Gubernia, Belarus. He was married twice: First to a woman named Sarah and then a second time to a woman named Bracha. Gregory Rutstein and Sarah had the following children: (i) Zena Rutstein, born in Tolochin, Belarus. She died in 1951. She married Theodore Chefitz; (ii) Fayga Rutstein was born in 1916 in Tolochin, Belarus. She died in 1984 in Moscow, Russia. She married Lazer Molchadsky in Moscow, Russia. He was born about 1916 in Moscow, Russia. He was murdered in 1941 during the Second World War, somewhere in Russia; (3) Gregory Rutstein II was born in 1918 in Tolochin, Belarus. He died on December 2, 1999 in Chicago, Illinois. He married Tanya Yurevckih.

When World War One started, Gregory Rutstein I went to war and was badly wounded. He died in or around 1916. His wife, Bracha, died from famine and a broken heart a few years later. Their children – two girls and a boy were taken to a special Jewish orphanage in Moscow and never returned to Tolochin.

Israel Rothstein and Yaakov Rutstein returned to Tolochin in 1933. They reportedly came looking for their nieces and nephew. News of their search eventually reached the children at their orphanage in Moscow and the children were devastated that they were not found. Ship manifests confirm that Yaakov Rutstein returned to the United States from Europe on September 29, 1933. The author met a Rutstein cousin in Israel, Boris Rutstein, that remembered Yaakov Rutstein visiting Tolochin as a child.

Gregory Rutstein II became a doctor and went to fight the Nazis during the Second World War. During the war, the whole village of Tolochin was burned down and almost the entire Jewish community was exterminated. Gregory Rutstein II resisted and fought the Nazis valiantly for four years and signed his name on the wall of the Nazi Military Commanding Center in 1945.

Being in Moscow, Gregory and his sister survived the war, but no other family members who remained in Tolochin did. After the fall of the Soviet Union, the descendants of Gregory I migrated to the United States. According to Edward Molchadsky, Gregory Rutstein II spoke about his uncles "who went to America in the 1910s to look for a better life." On his deathbed, Gregory II's dying wish to Edward Molchadsky and his other relatives was that they leave Russia and reconnect with their American cousins. After a century of separation, they have finally granted his wish.

5. NISSON (NATHAN) RUTSTEIN was born in 1885/1887 in Tolochin, Belarus. He died on July 17, 1931 in Brooklyn, New York. He married his first cousin, Fradie Rutstein. She was born on January 31, 1886 in Kochanova, Mogilev Gubernia, Belarus. She died on December 28, 1967 in Brooklyn, New York. According to Milton Rothstein, Nathan Rutstein, like Behr, was a powerful man. His strength was recalled by some of the Russian and Polish lumber workers in his father Jacob's (Yaakov's) lumber yard in Brooklyn.

The couple had three children: (i) Bertha Rutstein was born in 1914 in New York. She died in California. She married Gene Martinez. He was born in 1900 and also died in California. The couple had no children; (ii) Helen Rutstein was born in December 1916 in Brooklyn, New York. She died in December 1981 in Fort Lauderdale, Broward County, Florida. She married David Newmark in 1939 in New York City. He was born on October 10, 1911 in New York City, New York. He died in March 1984; (iii) Sylvia Rutstein was born in 1917 in Brooklyn, New York. She died in 1966 in Washington, DC. She married Harry Kozlow on 12 June 1946 in Maryland. He was born on August 04, 1914 in Brooklyn, New York.

6. SHIMON YESHAYA "SAMUEL" ROTHSTEIN was born about 1890 in Tolochin, Mogilev Guberniya, Belarus. He died in 1921 in New York, three months after the death of his mother, Riva. Samuel married Ida Edelson. She was born in around 1887 in Minsk, Belarus. She died in New York. Sam Rothstein and Ida Edelson had the following children: (i) Ann Rothstein was born on January 29, 1917 in Brooklyn, New York. She married Feivel David Belkind on August 28, 1938 in Brooklyn, New York. He was born on February 18, 1918 in Massachusetts; (ii) Shirley Rothstein was born on March 04, 1921 in Brooklyn, New York. She died in 1983 in New York. She married Arthur Hollander who also died in New York.

Anne Rutstein writes in a 1982 letter to Nancy Remz, "[m]y father Samuel (Sam) Rothstein, we never used Rut spelling, had a brother Jacob Rutstein, Ruthstein, etc. of Prudential Lumber Co. Also, brother Izzie, brother Nissen, and sister Frieda Boyarin. Jake or Jacob Rutstein being well to do, took care of my mom and her two girls. Shirley, my sister was 9 mos. and I was 4 yrs. old [when] my dad died in 1921. Helen, Bobbie, and Sylvia all lived on Rockaway Parkway. Frieda and Mendel Boyarin lived on the next block. Their daughter, Bessie Markowitz, is still around at 82 plus. There are still lumber companies in business related to the family-like Queen Lumber, Axinn Lumber, etc."

7. YISRAEL NACHUM ISRAEL ISADORE "IZZY" RUTSTEIN was born on January 1, 1894 in Tolochin, Mogilev Guberniya, modern-day Belarus. He died on March 14, 1963 in Brooklyn, New York. He married Lena. She was born around 1908 in New York. According to Ann Rutstein, Isidore Rutstein worked for Jacob Rutstein. Israel Rothstein was married twice. With his first wife, Lena, he had the following known children: (i) Rubin Rothstein was born about 1922 in New York; (ii) Bernard Rothstein was born about 1919 in New York. With his second wife, he had (iii) Natalie Rothstein

who was born about 1938 in New York; (iv) and possibly a fourth child. According to Ann Rutstein, Isadore worked for Jacob Rutstein at his lumber yard.

Some of Dov Behr's children are reported to have remained behind in Belarus. Two of Dov Behr's children died from diseases. Archival research reveals the following additional adult children:

1. Chana Rutstein
2. Devorah "Dviera" Rutstein (d. 1909/1910?)
3. Merka Rutstein
4. Etka Rutstein

Acknowledgments

The narrative takes the previous family trees and narratives authored by Milton Rothstein, Alan Redstone, Nancy Wexler, and others, with my additions synthesizes them into a single historical narrative. There are no doubt many errors in this history, but it should still give the reader a general sense of who these people were, what their lives were like, and inspire their descendants to carry on their positive legacies. A special thank you needs to be expressed to Nancy Wexler who first took me at the age of sixteen to the New York City archives and shared with me the art of archival genealogical research. Members of the Tolochin Rutstein family have spelled the surname as follows: Rothstein, Rutstein, Rotstein, Rootshtein, Rotchstein, and Rutshtein and many other variants. The author is of the opinion that most Rothsteins (the variety of spelling is of no genealogical significance) are not related to this family. The author, however, has come across a number of Rothsteins in his research who are also from the province of Minsk, and are seemingly related. This is especially true of those Rothsteins that originate from the vicinity of Orsha and Tolochin. Looking at many records in the archives, seeing the repetition of family names, it became clear that there was an unknown Rothstein progenitor, perhaps the father or grandfather of Nachum Rutstein, who initially adopted the surname, and which over time produced many different branches of the family throughout the greater Tolochin area.

PART IV

BIOGRAPHY OF JACOB "J.R." RUTSTEIN

Yaakov or "Yankel" or "Yankev" or "Jacob" or "J.R." Rutstein was born on the 15th of April, 1878[37] to Dov Behr Rutstein and Riva Rothstein in Tolochin, in the *guberniya* of Mogilev, which was then the region of White Russia of the Russian Empire and what is today known as Belarus. Legend provides that Yankel came from a materially and culturally poor family who eked out a living in the Tolochin countryside[38].

The proximity of the railway to the village of Tolochin made its mark on the economic life and occupation of people in the village, including the Rutstein family. The Tolochin markets and seasonal fairs were a defining feature of Yaakov's childhood. At the age of six, Dov Behr, Yaakov's father, took him to the farmers and commodities market and also to the seasonal fairs. Shprintsy (Sophia) Lvovna Rohkind (1903-2000), in her unpublished memoirs, and Oleg Plaksitsky, in his "Our Talachynshchyna: The Grit of Time" (March 5, 2005), capture the scene which Yaakov would have experienced at the Tolochin market and its seasonal fairs at the dawn of the 20th Century. The following composite description provides that:

> *Tolochin's fairs were held annually on May 9 - "Nikolaevskaya," on July 20 - "Ilinskaya" and on September 8 - "Uspenskaya." Peasants from the surrounding villages brought to market their products and services. Sellers and buyers came not only from the surrounding villages and towns but also from Orsha and Mogilev. They brought with them vegetables, hay, firewood, and wooden and linen products. The peasants also brought pigs, piglets, and various birds for sale and sold them immediately at the*

---

[37] Different dates of birth are found in different records. Alternative dates are 1876 and 1877.

[38] This is related by Ruth Paretzky Hershkovitz. Her view must be stated that it was in comparison to the Paretzky family into which Yaakov would eventually marry. It should be further noted that Jacob's grandfather, Nachum, had been a wealthy man.

carts. They sold, in addition to agricultural goods, poultry, cows, sheep, goats, horses, cloth, dishes, harness, household goods, while many gypsies and visitors roamed around the horses.

At the fairs, one could hear spoken Belarusian, Yiddish, Russian, Polish, Gypsy, Lithuanian, Latvian, and German. Everybody understood each other perfectly.

For the peasants from the surrounding villages, the fairs were an opportunity to sell produce in the marketplace, and for artisans to sell their goods to the same peasants. Those who were richer, made wholesale purchases, and then sold what they bought in other places, at other fairs, and had their own cooks. People were waiting for the fair, as they would wait for a holiday; it was an opportunity to meet and talk.

At the fairs, the village girls came in elegant dresses with ribbons in their hair. They walked around the bazaar and the streets with flowers in their hands. The guys played harmonies, drank from the monopoly and sellers of vodka and drinks. There were quite a lot of drunks. Sometimes there were fights, but never any serious carnage. Everything was under the undisturbed eye of the police in the person of a local officer and guard. It was noisy and fun. There was a brisk trade. Everyone called customers to himself and touted his goods. After a successful purchase or sale, people went to the tavern for a glass of wine or something stronger to consolidate a bargain.

At the markets, Yankel met diverse types of people who came to Tolochin to buy goods from other places. From early childhood, Yankel developed expertise in furs, hides, bristles, and hog hair. Yankel dealt with the Russian peasants buying various items such as horsehair (bristles), produce, furs, and pelts. During Yankel's school days, he was engaged in many business activities and engaged in games such as *waldsacher* (an estimation of crops prior to harvest for trade). For example, Yankev could look at an apple farm or wheat or anything grown and accurately forecast the amount of fruit or grain to be harvested.

Yankel anticipated with great excitement accompanying his father, Dov Behr, to market and the seasonal fairs. According to Milton Rothstein, Yankel was a child genius who, even in early adolescence, exceeded his father's business prowess. By the time Yankel was twelve, he had developed such an acute business prowess that he would go to market and the annual fairs and return with more goods and money than his father, Dov Behr. It wasn't unusual for Yaakov to go to the market and return with three times the amount of money than that of Dov Behr. According to Jay Rothstein, father and son competed with one another regarding who could make more money.

Yankel went to *heder*, or Jewish school, until the age of twelve but was otherwise self-educated. Yaakov employed his Jewish knowledge by serving as a *hazan* cantor and *shliach tzibur* leader of the congregation at the *bima* altar of the synagogue. Once, Yankel was *en route* to synagogue for high holiday services and came across a blacksmith working. The work of the blacksmith so intrigued the young and curious Yaakov that he stood and watched the blacksmith in awe. As the hours passed, the high holiday services progressed and Yankel did not attend synagogue. Dov Ber, upset that his son missed services, gave Yankel a lashing that left him with a permanent scar. Yankel vowed to himself that he would never hit his or any children—a vow he kept.

Like many of the Rutstein men, many of whom were cantors *chazzanim*, Yaakov had an excellent voice and was musically inclined. As a child and young man, Yankel was known in town for his beautiful voice and he was asked to lead the prayers as a *hazan* in the synagogue. But at some point in his youth, likely during his teenage years, Yankel damaged his vocal cords and voice by drinking vinegar (which had a similar intoxicating effect to alcohol). Yaakov continued to sing, but his voice was never the same.

Yaakov is Drafted into Military Service

Yaakov was drafted into the Russian army as a (young) teenager. Milton[39] Rothstein relates a story about Yankev which occurred to him as a young man after being drafted into the Russian army but prior to his departure. Milton writes:

My father's grandmother was a psychic. She knew by a 6th sense or godly powers of what was going on 1,000 miles away. She knew when so and so had a child, or a loved one passed away. In this time period, the 1850 – 1900 era, there were no TV, radio, or newspapers in Russia. Jacob's grandmother was worshipped by her family and especially my father, Jacob. Jacob tells a story of when he was leaving for the army, she told him thusly, "you are young to be in such a city and you will be on X street [which she described exactly] and two thugs will attempt to kill you. Now listen to my warning and remember this as it is going to save your life." Sure enough, when Jacob was in this town, he was walking in a street and the place looked familiar [according to the description of his grandmother] he suddenly remembered his grandmother's warning in time. Minutes later, two muggers attempted to kill and rob J.R. but

---

[39] Elsewhere Milton writes: "[Yankel's] grandmother was a psychic [] [whereby she would predict] many events happening long distances away such as births and deaths reported on the day it happened. Weeks later official confirmation by a letter followed. [Yankel] recalls that before he went into the army, she warned him about a street in a city where he was going to be and that he would be attacked by two goslonim [thugs]. She described every detail of the attack and the surroundings. He said this occurred [exactly how she said] and because of his grandmother's warning he was able to protect himself [and] save his life."

Jay Rothstein, Milton's son, tells nearly an identical story about Yankel but identifies not Yankel's grandmother as the psychic but rather Yankel's mother. According to Jay Rothstein, Yankel was set to travel from town to town and Riva had a dream that he would be attacked or killed in a specific town and a specific place. Before Yankel left on his journey, she warned him of this upcoming attack. It happened that Yankel had to travel through this town and place that his mother described. When he found himself in the location his mother had warned him about, the attack came and he was able to defend himself and he wasn't hurt or killed.

he was alert and strong and beat them off & escaped with his life[40]."

According to Jay Rothstein, Yankel learned to play the drums in the army and served as a barabanchick or "drummer boy." He was praised by his comrades for being an excellent drummer. After Yankel's discharge from the army, Yankel was hired by a German company to export seafood and lumber from Russia into Western Europe. By the age of eighteen years, he was appointed to serve as the General Manager of the company's operations in the East. Yankel may have spent several years during the 1890s in this position. Yankel was very successful and managed to accumulate a small fortune that he deposited in London, United Kingdom, possibly in anticipation of future emigration[41].

Yaakov Decides to Leave His Homeland

It appears that Yaakov began contemplating leaving Russia near the turn of the 19th century. At the turn of the century, a wave of pogroms swept the region including a minor pogrom in 1899 and/or 1900 within Tolochin, which saw the destruction of Jewish life and property. Moreover, by 1902, tensions between the Russian Empire and the Empire of Japan began to increase over rival imperial ambitions in Manchuria and Korea. These conditions motivated Yaakov and some of his relatives to leave the land of their birth. According to Ruth Paretzky Hershkovitz, Yankel departed Tolochin together with Mendel Boyarin, his brother-in-law, Mordechai Shmuel (Max) Paretzky, and Yankov (Jacob) Poretzky, future brother-in-laws, to seek a better life in America.

---

[40] Or pre-teen.

[41] According to Rita Rutstein Kaplan, during this time period, and prior to his immigration to the United States, Yaakov had failed 'marriage discussions' regarding someone in Russia. It is likely that the Soloveitchik Shadchan Letter dates to this period.

Events, however, transpired that would prevent the group from arriving in the United States at the same time. During his journey to the United States, Yaakov suffered from rheumatic fever[42]. The medical condition (which was likely never fully medically treated) seriously damaged Yaakov's heart and he would suffer for the remainder of his life[43]. Yaakov is reported to have checked into a hospital in London where he reportedly stayed bedridden for months—although he may at times have also worked as a tailor and presser of clothing in a local sweatshop. According to Milton Rothstein, Yaakov's stay in London was reported to have been extended but at a minimum of many months. Yaakov is reported to have arrived in London with $800 in cash, the equivalent of $20,000 in 2015 money. The medical expenses associated with his illness depleted his life savings[44]. The whole experience, lacking access to affordable healthcare, alone, in a strange land, with his life savings depleted, was severely traumatic and would be one that Yaakov would never forget, and in many ways come to shape the course of his life. With his savings depleted, Yaakov attempted to complete his immigration to the United States. However, upon arrival in the United States, the sickly Yaakov was deported back to London and eventually to Russia.

Upon his return to Russia, Yaakov encountered a society in chaos. A series of anti-Jewish pogroms was sweeping the Russian Empire, including within the Tolochin region, leaving thousands of dead Jews and many more wounded. The New York Times described a pogrom, which were typical of the era, and which occurred during Easter of 1903:

The anti-Jewish riots in Kishinev, Bessarabia are worse than the censor will permit to publish. There was a well laid-out plan for the general massacre of Jews on the day following the Orthodox

---

[42] Another account states that Yaakov also/alternatively had an eye infection.

[43] Milton Rothstein, however, observed, that although Jacob suffered throughout his life, "I never heard him even mention it once. He was a real man and a soldier to the end."

[44] In one account, all that remained was a few small diamonds. Jay Rothstein disagrees with this narrative. "I was not aware of his having had rheumatic heart or being sent back to Russia. All I recall hearing from my father O"H was that it was a disorder of his eyes, was treated successfully, and he continued to NY, though penniless. The $800 is the savings I recall as well, attributed to his savings from his work as the General Manager for Forest Products for the German trading company."

Easter. The mob was led by priests and the general cry, "Kill the Jews" was taken up all over the city. The Jews were taken wholly unaware and were slaughtered like sheep. The dead numbered 120 and the injured about 500. The scenes of horror attending this massacre are beyond description. Babies were literally torn to pieces by the frenzied and bloodthirsty mob. The local police made no attempt to check the reign of terror. At sunset, the streets were piled with corpses and wounded. Those who could make their escape fled in terror and the city is now practically deserted of Jews.

At the same time, tensions resulted in open conflict between the Russian Empire and the Empire of Japan between February 1904 and September 1905. The conflict became known as the Russo-Sino (Japanese) war. Yaakov was drafted into the Russian army where he served as an instructor for new recruits in the army.[45] While in the army, Yankel experienced anti-Semitism from his peers and superiors. In one instance, another soldier [in one version, a senior officer] insulted Yaakov because he was Jewish [by calling him, among other things, a "*zhid*," a derogatory term for a Jew, akin to "Jew Bastard" in English]. Yaakov slapped the man across the face [in one version, punched or slugged the man in the face]. At the subsequent military tribunal and court-martial, Yaakov was pardoned by the court because he was provoked and acted in a fit of religious passion and therefore was not at fault. The result surprised many as such act was normally unforgivable in the czar's army.

At the conclusion of the Russian-Japanese War, Yaakov encountered a new wave of regional pogroms that swept the greater Minsk region including Tolochin and Orsha where over 40 Jewish people were killed. With no obvious future for himself, Yaakov departed the Russian Empire, and in 1905

---

[45] Jay Rothstein disagrees with this sequence of events. He writes, "Jacob escaped from Russia *before* being drafted a second time to avoid such draft." [emphasis mine] It's possible that he initially arrived in 1902, was deported back to London (and Russia), and then to avoid the draft immigrated in 1904. Two census reports place his emigration in 1904. This needs further research.

arrived on the shores of Manhattan Island with, according to Ruth Paretzky Hershkovitz, "only a rope to hold up his pants[46]."

Yaakov Rutstein Forges A New Life in A New World, Marries & Raises A Family

Whatever the precise year of Yaakov's emigration and whatever his precise economic status upon arrival, Yaakov, in his mid-twenties, began a new life in America. According to Alan Redstone and Milton Rothstein, upon Yankel's immigration, he settled on the Lower East Side of Manhattan. From approximately 1905 to 1909[47], Yankel pressed clothes in a sweatshop for sixteen hours a day earning three dollars a week.

The capital of Jewish America at the turn of the century was New York's Lower East Side. This densely packed district of tenements, factories, and docklands had long been a starting point for recent immigrants. Hundreds

---

[46] There are inconsistent narratives regarding whether Jacob was drafted once or twice into the Russian army, whether he saw service in the Russian-Japanese war and what year he immigrated to the United States. It does appear, in the opinion of the author, that Yankel was drafted twice into the Russian army but the oral history in this regard is inconsistent and ambiguous and it is possible he was only drafted once. Further, it's unclear whether the first time Yankel was drafted as a child or rather as a teenager--although one version of the story makes it appear as if this occurred when he was a child, perhaps as a teenager of twelve or thirteen. It is also possible that he was drafted as an adult. It's also unclear whether Yaakov actually saw service in the Russo-Japanese war or left prior to its commencement, during the war or after the war. According to Milton Rothstein, Yaakov left Russia during the war. According to different census reports, Yaakov immigrated either in 1904 or 1905 which confirm Milton's account. One journalistic account, however, places his emigration before the war in 1902 and another oral history account after the war in 1906. A review of ship records is inconclusive with two entries for a Jacob Rothstein, possibly the same person, in 1906 and one entry for a Jacob Rothstein in 1902. According to one story that supports the 1902 account, Yaakov sensed that he was to be drafted into the army, and having served once, he preemptively avoided the draft by attempting to emigrate to the United States. In reconciling the 1902 and 1906 immigration dates, the author posits that Yaakov may have been deported back to London (and/or Russia) after a 1902 arrival and then immigrated a second time in 1906. According to Ruth Paretzky Hershkovitz, Yaakov came to America penniless with only a "rope to hold up his pants." According to another report, however, Yaakov came to the United States with a couple of diamonds representing the remainder of whatever wealth he had accumulated in Europe. The current above-the-line section is the author's attempt to reconcile the apparently conflicting narratives.

[47] Possibly as early as 1902 depending on which version of the story is adopted.

of thousands of the new Jewish arrivals from Eastern Europe settled there on arrival. When Yankel first set foot on the Lower East Side, he stepped into a Jewish world. The earliest Eastern European Jews to settle there had quickly established synagogues, mutual-aid societies, libraries, and stores. Every major institution, from the bank to the grocery store to the social club to the neighborhood bookmaker, was Jewish-owned or Jewish-run. Everyone a Jewish immigrant might speak to in the course of daily business would likely be Jewish. Even the owners of the garment factories and department stores, where many immigrants worked, were Jewish. For Yankel, this immersion in a familiar world, around people who shared a common language, faith, and background, was profoundly reassuring. For all the comfort that this shared heritage brought, however, the Lower East Side was still a very difficult place to live—and a crowded one. By the year 1900, the district was packed with more than 700 people per acre, making it the most crowded neighborhood on the planet. The reformer Jacob Riis described a visit to a typical tenement building occupied by Eastern European Jewish families:

I have found in three rooms father, mother, twelve children, and six boarders. They sleep on the half-made clothing for beds. I found out that several people slept in a subcellar four feet by six, on a pile of clothing that was being made[48].

This congestion brought many hazards with it, along with many annoyances. Nearly half of the city's deaths by fire took place on the Lower East Side. Disease was rampant, clean water was hard to come by, and privacy was unheard of. For many immigrant children, their education in American life was acquired in the city streets, where lovers strolled amid streams of raw sewage, vendors offered almost anything for sale, con artists and petty thieves worked the crowds, and horse carriages burdened with goods clogged the muddy roadways. The Lower East Side could certainly be frightening, dangerous, noisy, and cramped. However, it was still a place of relative safety compared to the virulently anti-Semitic Russian Empire. And, however

---

[48] The Century Illustrated Monthly Magazine, Volume 21; Volume 43, edited by Josiah Gilbert Holland, Richard Watson Gilder, p. 327.

chaotic it might be, as some observers at the time noted, it was still the greatest concentration of Jewish life in nearly two thousand years.

Most of the new Jewish immigrants faced unique challenges in their search for work. Yankel would have been no exception. In the Russian Empire, Jews had been barred by law from a wide range of jobs, including farming, which brought a more limited set of skills with them than some immigrants did. At the same time, Jews had to overcome the prejudices of U.S. employers, where "gentlemen's agreements" and open bigotry prevented them from entering the professions and many heavy industrial jobs. As Yankel learned the landscape of the Lower East Side, he adopted the American name Jacob or Jake, perhaps partly to easily fit into his new homeland. Jacob eventually became known affectionately as "J.R." or Jay R.

Jewish immigrants like J.R. often had to find employment outside of the more established trades, as well as create opportunities for themselves between the cracks of the American economy. More than one-half of all Eastern European Jewish immigrants worked in manual occupations, predominantly in the garment industry. The Jewish neighborhoods of New York were home to countless tiny, airless sweatshop factories, where women, teenagers, and children worked long hours cutting, sewing, and finishing clothing for pennies per piece. A reporter for The Century visited some of the garment workers of New York and described the conditions which Jacob encountered at the turn of the century:

> *The Jewish sweatshop workers toil from six in the morning until eleven at night. Fifty cents as compensation for these murderous hours are not unusual. Trousers at 84 cents per dozen, 8 cents for a round coat, and 10 cents for a frock coat, are labor prices that explain the sudden affluence of heartless merchant manufacturers, and the biting poverty of miserable artisans[49].*

---

[49] Id.

The precise impetus for J.R. to leave the sweatshops of the Lower East Side and find other types of work is shrouded in mystery. Perhaps it was because of J.R.'s anticipated marriage to Basha "Bessie" Poretzky in September 1908, and the obvious need to escape the horrid conditions of the Lower East Side. Whatever his motivations, it was Jacob's sense of curiosity and intuition, the same childlike awe that he expressed watching the blacksmith, which provided him with his next opportunity. According to Milton Rothstein:

> On Sundays [J.R.] would travel around the city by foot [because] he didn't want to spend a nickel for [the] trolley. And he would watch the wreckers of old homes and industrial sites. [And from this he] learned the basics of [what would become over time] his new career. [J.R.] saved up a few dollars [and] became a boss wrecker.

After earlier failed marriage negotiations, Yaakov and Basha Poretzky opened marriage discussions. Basha Poretzky was the daughter of a respected rabbi in Tolochin and her brothers had been friends to Jacob. It is reported that Jacob Rutstein and Basha knew one another while they both lived in Tolochin. However, according to Milton Rothstien, they only became involved with one another in the United States. The couple married on September 17, 1908, in Brooklyn, New York. However, according to Ruth Paretzky Hershkovitz, while the marriage was not formalized in Tolochin, it was in Tolochin where discussions of their marriage first were conceptualized.

Evidence suggests that Jacob had relocated from the Lower East Side to Brownsville, Brooklyn as early as 1909, perhaps out of a desire to provide a softer and safer environment for his new wife. According to Milton Rothstein, Jacob had been in the United States for some time[50] when Basha, who was nine or ten years[51] his junior, arrived. According to Milton

---

[50] Milton provides that Jay R. had been in the United States for eight years when Basha arrived and married Jacob. This is a reference which supports the account of a 1902 immigration, not a 1906 migration. Either way, this number cannot be accurate.

[51] Other records suggest that there was only a four- or five-year age gap between them.

Rothstein, the "romance was short, and they were married in Brownsville where my brother [and] two sisters were born." According to Ruth Paretzky Hershkovitz, the marriage between Yaakov and Basha "was not a love marriage" and it "must have been arranged." Ruth Paretzky Hershkovitz was given the impression that, at the time of the marriage, there was a sense among the Paretzky family that Bessie could have done better than Jacob—his being both culturally and financially inferior. Basha was the daughter of a Rabbi who was refined and elegant—and according to Helaine Blumenfeld stemmed from a long line of Talmudic scholars. According to Ruth Paretzky Hershkovitz, Jacob had been perceived in Europe as a "prust" person (e.g. like a villager) and had in the New World sought to make himself more refined. This *"prust"* persona was true in contrast to his wife, Bessie, who carried herself like she was a queen and was elegant and wore very nice clothing. According to Ruth Paretzky Hershkovitz, Jacob Rutstein's vast ambitions were motivated, in part, to prove to his in-laws, and Bessie's family, that he was a good match.

Upon moving to Brownsville, Jacob and Bessie started a family. Their first child, Bertha Rutstein, was born on July 28, 1909 in Brooklyn, New York. Nathan (Nachum) Rothstein was born on April 13, 1911 in Brooklyn, New York. Dora (Dvora) Rothstein was born on September 10, 1913.

Bessie Poretzky and Jacob Rutstein. Brooklyn, New York.
Circa 1907–1910.

Jacob Makes A Living

Few facts exist about Jacob between 1911 and 1925. However, it was during this period that Jacob accumulated his fortune that would one day reach into the millions of dollars.

On March 25, 1912, the Triangle Shirtwaist factory fire occurred, nearly half of the 146 workers killed were Jewish teenage girls, one of whom was Emma Rootstein (no known relation). This event would be a pivotal moment in the history of the labor movement and no doubt played a role in Jay R.'s psyche—perhaps confirming to Jacob that his career working in a sweatshop was over. On April 4, 1911, Nisson Rutstein and Israel Rutstein immigrated to the United States on a ship named the Kursk, both sponsored by Jacob Rutstein. The listed contact in their country of origin was Berka Rutstein, Jacob's father. Their point of contact in New York was Jacob Rutstein, who was then living at 744 Rockaway Avenue in Brooklyn, New York.

By 1912, historical records reference in the American Lumberman, a national trade magazine, showed the formation of the Brownsville Housewrecking Corporation. Its purpose, in addition to house demolition, was to deal in lumber. The authorized capital for the company was $1,200 which is approximately $30,000 in 2019 dollars. Jacob's co-partners were listed as Max Poretzky, his brother-in-law, and Aaron Entee(n). According to Milton Rothstein, Jacob's "great business acumen made him successful from his first job." Nevertheless, Jacob did much to develop his skillset. According to Milton Rothstein, Jacob learned the wrecking business from careful observation of work sites on the weekends. Jacob also took jobs outside of his comfort zone. He took one job in Spencer Frank Park in Saratoga Springs, New York which made him a few thousand dollars.

This created opportunity and some luck. According to Milton Rothstein, Jacob's workers uncovered a small cache of money in one demolition job which at the time was a fortune of seven or eight hundred dollars. He gave each worker a small reward for their honesty in not keeping the money[52]. Jacob invested the money back into his businesses.

According to Alan Redstone, in addition to becoming a wrecker of buildings, Jacob also opened up a second-hand lumber business with the old lumber he salvaged from the demolition sites. According to Milton Rothstein, Jacob "watched every detail [of the business]." "J.R.'s interest to make money was well founded. Number one, to save pennies meant eventually to save dollars. When he had the second-hand lumber yard, he instructed the men to save the rusty nails which when accumulated brought in a few dollars." Jacob "prospered and soon he started selling new lumber" in a new company.

As Jacob's wealth accumulated, Jacob become slowly involved in buying and selling real estate and then in property development. According to Milton Rothstein, "he was a cracker-jack builder just from observing the apartment house operations by our customers." During this time period, he also brought property on Rockaway Avenue between Jerome and Riverdale, a big house at Twenty-Seven Tapscott Street near the Eastern Parkway section of Brownsville, and other properties. At the same time, Jacob began acquiring real estate throughout Brooklyn.

This period shows two photographs of Jacob with his brother in-laws, likely taken during a visit to America by his father-in-law, Rabbi Tzvi Hirsch Poretzky(n).

---

[52] According to Jay Rothstein, it was closer to $2,000.

From Left to Right: Rabbi Zvi Hirsch Poretzky(n), Max Poretzk), Jacob Poret, Jacob Rutstein, Nathan Poretzky. Brooklyn, New York. Circa 1912.

From top Left to Right standing: Anna and Max Poretsky, Nathan Poretzky, Anna Poret, Bessie Poretzky Rutstein. Middle row from left to right, sitting: Rabbi Zvi Hirsch Poretzky(n), Jacob Poret with infant son Frank Poret, Jacob Rutstein. Row of children from left to right: unknown, unknown, Sidney Poretzky? Nicky Rutstein, Bertha Rutstein. Brooklyn, New York, circa 1913.

In April 1914, Jacob became a founding member of Adas Israel of Brownsville, a local charitable and Zionist organization. The 1915, New York City census lists Jacob living with his mother, wife, and children. His occupation is listed as a plumber. In 1916, Jacob learned that the New York Telephone company wanted land which he owned. When the phone company approached Jacob to purchase the land, he refused to sell it to them. The company approached him several more times, each time increasing their offer until they offered several times what the land was worth. Jacob's second son, Morris Milton Rothstein, was born on July 28, 1916 in Brooklyn, Kings County, New York.

In or around 1917, Jacob was stricken with tuberculosis and he was forced to retire to a sanitarium in upstate New York where he spent ten months recuperating. The three Yiddish letters, annexed to this document below, between Bessie and Jacob date from this period.

Letter from Bessie to Jacob – August 23, 1917

האַרשענצעענדער ענד ליבען דער
טאַייערער געוואָאהל. יעקב
ראַטשטיין לעב וואָאהל גליקלעך
איך דיא קינדער גיפֿונען זיך לייב
גאָט גיזונדט גיבלייען פֿון דיר גוטעס
צוהערין יעקב איך קען נישט
פֿאַרשטיין דיין פּאָליטיג וואָרום דו
שרייבסט נישט דא. בעסער איז
אלעס וואַרט ...ווען איך ווייס אז
דו גיפֿינסט זיך פֿאָלקאַממען גיזונד
וואָאלט מיר ניט גיאַרט איך ווייס
אַז א שיי קאָלאפֿין האָט ניט קיין
ווערדע ענד דיא קינדער אויך דיא
זעלבע. יעקב שרייב מיר פֿון אלעס
וואָס טוט זיך מיט דיר ענד וויא
פֿילסטע אין גיזונד. דא איז קיינע
נייס.

Respected and beloved, the wonderfully dear Yaakov Rothstein, live well, and be lucky. I, and the children, find ourselves, thank God, healthy. It was good to hear from you, Yaakov. I can't understand your position because you do not write here, it is better every word. When I would know that you were fully healthy, it would not bother me. I know that a *shklapin* has no worth and the same goes for the children [and myself]. Yaakov, write to me all that is happening with you and how you are feeling in your health. Here, there is no news.

אין יאד גיי איך ניט ענד וויל ניט וויסין פון אים. דעם ערשטין לעטער מיט דעם צעק האב איך גיבראכט אין יאד

I do not go to the Yad and do not want to know of him. The first letter with the check I brought to the Yad.

האט מיר ענטין גיגעבין א צעק 35 דאלער ענד מער ניט איך דיינק אזוי צאל דיא הויז פייטון ענד דיא הויז אין ווינטער איז ניט גוט.

And Entin gave me a check of 35 dollars and no more. I am thinking to pay to paint the house, and the house is not good in the winter.

דיא קינדער לאזון דיר גריסין פריינדלאך זיי ווילין זעהען דעם פאפין מיישע מיריל וועמען ער דערזעט אין ווינדע שרייט ער פאפא.

The children send their friendly regards. They want to see their Papa. Moshe Michel [Milton] looks out the window and cries out for his Papa.

ביטע צו שרייבען פון אלעס איך האב דיר גישרייבען אין א לעטער דאס איך פיל ניט גוט יעצט דיא זעלבע צו קיין דאקטער גיי איך ניט ענד אזוי בלייבט דאס וואס האב איך צו פערלירין...

Please write from everything. I have written to you in a letter that I do not feel good, and it still remains the same. To a doctor, I do not go, and that is how it remains. What do I have to lose?

פערבלייב גיזונד ענד פערברייינג פריי ענד גליקליך

Stay well and spend your time free and with good luck.

Basha   Basha

Letter from Bessie to Jacob – August 27, 1917

מאנטאג , August 27ᵗʰ   Monday, August 27

הארגעשעצטער ענד פיל געליבטער געוואהל ,יעקב ראטשטיין לעב וואהל.

My dear and beloved Yaakov Rothstein, live and be well.

איך די קינדער געפינען זיך לייב גאט גיזונד גיבען פון דיר גוטעס צוהערן. יעקב פרעקס צו פארין אין

I, and the children, find ourselves, thank God, healthy. It was nice to hear from

דיא מאנטעס יע דו קענסט פארון
איך בין ניט דיין דאייע .ענד דו
דארפסט ניט פרעגין דאס וואס דו
מוסט פארענד פארברייינג גוט דיא
צייט ענד ועד געזונד אז דו זאלסט
נאך קענען גיפונען דיין לעבענס
באגלייטערין   נאך   דאיינע
געדאיינקען זורג ניט אלעס ועט
אליין קומען

עס איס קיינע נייס .שיים בא ראכין
איז ארויס פריי פון מיליטער .ניסין
זיין געליבטער פרוי איז גיקומען .
דיין גאנצע מישפאכא איז גיזונד
דאיינע ליבע מישע שוועגערינס ענד
פאמיליעס זיינען נאך ניט גיקומען

פארבלייב גיזונד ענד פאר אין דיא
מאנטיס אויב דיר פעלט געלט
שרייב ועט מען דיר שיקין איך
האב בא ענטענן קיין געלט ניט
גינומען האט גידארפט קיין געלט
אין דיא בענק ניט פעלין נאר
האיינט ועל איך צוגיין נאך געלט
ווייל מדארף .דיא הויז פייטין .
שרייב דיא אדרעס ווען דו ועסט
קומען אין קאנטרע דו זאלט ניט
וואגין קומען יעצט האיים וואס
גוט

דו האסט שיים ניט וואס צו
פארלירין   דאיינע   גאלדענע
גשעפטין וואס דיין ענטין מאכט
יעצט קאנסטע דערמאנען באשעס
רייד .אדיא ענד ענטפער גלייך
דאיינע קינדער גיריסין דיר
פריינדלאך בריינע נאכום דארע
מישע מירעלע ער גייט שיים אליין
אין גוטע שאה

-- he [now] walks on his own! May it be in an auspicious time!

Basha   Basha

איך וועל דיר מער קיין לעטערס
ניט שרייבען אהער אייך נא איז
שפעסיל

P.S. I will no longer send letters if it is not special.

Letter from Bessie to Jacob — August 27, 1917

August 27th   August 27

טרייער יעקב לעב וואהל גליקלעך
איך דיא קינדער גיפונען זיך לייב
גאט גיזונד גיבען פון דיר גוטעס צו
הערין יעקב דיין לעטער יעצט
ערהאלטין ענד איר ענטפער דיר
גלייך אויב דיר איז אינטערעסינע
אין מיין ראט!

Dear Yaakov, live well and with good luck. I, and the children, find ourselves, thank God, healthy. It was good to hear from you. Yaakov, your letter I just now received, and I answer it immediately. If you are interested in my thoughts!

פאר אין דיא מאנטעס אויף דער
צייט וואס דו דארפסט 3-2 וואכין
דאס וואס דו האסט פערלאָרין אין
געלט קער איך ניט דאס וואס דו
האסט דיין גיזונד פערלאָרין ענד
מיינער צו גענומען דאס איז אפשר
ווערט ענד

Travel to the mountains for the time that you need, the 2-3 weeks. That you lost money in [making] money, I don't care. This that you have lost your health, and took mine away, this is possibly worthwhile. And this you will not easily be able to repay. I would give my advice that we remain no more from afar. This would be better for us and better for God...

צוריק דאס וועסטו פילאייכט ניט
אומקערען שיים איך וואלט דיר א
ראטין אז מיר זאלן אוממער זיין
פון דער ווייטען וואל גיווען בעסער
פאר אונז ענד בעסער פאר גאט ...
יעצט הייסטע מיר זוכען דינסטין

Now you are making me search for servants when there is none (funds) and for what to waste. Your good times were lacking from all enjoyments now when

ווען עס איז ניטא ענד פאר וואס
צונעמען דאיינע גוטע צייטין איז

גיוועז פארמאכט פון אלע
פארגעננוגענס יעצט ווען דו ביסט
קראנק ענד פון דערוויייטין
מיינסטע אויך ניט וואס צו שרייבין
ועל ריידון א פולע איז איבעריג
פאר און פערברייינג גוט דיא צייט
ענד ווער גיזונד לאז איבער דאיינע
בליענדע גידיינקען אויף דיא הויכע
בערג ...איך קען דיר שרייבען אז
מיישע מירעלע גייט שיים אליין גיב
גאט אין גוטע צייט ער זאל זיין
גיזונד ענד שייטארק. אלע גירוסין
דיר ברייינע נאכום דארע .זאיי
גיזונד ענד פאר גיזונד ענד קום
גיזונד דאס איז יעצט דיין גאנצער
אידיאל. צו ווערין גיזונד ענד
דערזעהן דיין גוטין כאראקטער איך
האב אויף גירופין

פריי ארויס איז ער בארואכין שעם
נייס באזונדערע קיינע מיליטער פון
פענטין איך ועל הויז דיא

you are sick and afar and yet you still do
not to write!

I have much to say but it is excessive.
Travel and spend the time well and get
well. Leave your blinded thoughts on the
high mountains... I can write to you that
Moshe Michel walks already, alone,
thank G-d. In good time he should be
healthy and strong. Everyone sends
regards Braina, Nachum, Dora. Be well
and travel healthy and return healthy this
is now your entire purpose. To get well
and return your good character.

I've called Baruch'n. He was released free
from the military. There is no other
news. I will paint the house.

Crown Heights

Jay R.'s cumulative successes led him to eventually become a multi-millionaire. The Rutsteins moved in Brooklyn from Brownsville to the wealthy Crown Heights. The Rutsteins lived in a mansion on 1388 President Street which was known as "millionaires' row." According to Milton Rothstein:

> *Ninety percent of the people from Kingston to New York Ave. [in Crown Heights] were enormously rich and were the elite of the era. There was such as Samuel Barnet, President of the Municipal Bank, David Issa, a premier apartments house builder, Samuel Rotenberg originator of Wool Co., and President of the Brooklyn Jewish Center. There was also Nathan D. Shapiro, lawyer and republican candidate for governor who was narrowly beaten by F.D. Roosevelt; Henry Gold, millionaire builder, as was B.J. Kline – also the owner of J. Kurtz furniture store owner. Next store was the Horowitz family who owned many properties including Long Beach's foremost hotel and the Treibity family, the owner of Treibity shoes and father of Dorothy Tree, number one communist actress in Hollywood. Nearby was also Irwin Steingart, democrat leader son, leader of the House of New York State, Stanley Steingart, and many others since forgotten.*

Milton Rothstein was the first child to come of age in Jacob and Bessie's new home. According to Marty Poretskin, the Rutsteins, due to Jacob's success in the lumber business, had a chauffeur, and a maid. Helaine Blumenfeld, however, presents a different view, that the Rutsteins were wealthy yet humble and simple. [53]Phyllis Birnbaum recalls, "I remember going [to visit Jacob Rutstein and his family] as a little girl and they all spoke in Yiddish [in their home] and I couldn't understand a word they said."

---

[53] This is at least in contrast to the family in which Nathan Rothstein, Jacob's son, eventually married into.

Milton Rothstein. Crown Heights, Brooklyn, New York. Circa 1919.

The Nominal Measurements Revolution & J.R.'s Career as a Real Estate Developer

The growth in the economy at the dawn of the roaring 1920s, and the increased demand for lumber, led Rutstein to acquire the raw source of timber. During the early 1920s, Rutstein began to acquire lumber fields throughout the United States and as far away as Oregon. By owning the source of lumber, Jay R. was able to sell cheap lumber at reduced rates and undercut his competition throughout New York City. This success evolved into the formation, in 1922, of the Brownsville Lumber Company. Jacob took his experience in the lumber industry, developed in Tolochin—which was known for its lumber industry—and used that while operating his latest businesses[54]. As Principal of Brownsville Lumber, Rutstein began to supply lumber to New York's leading real estate families and began to experiment with doing his own real-estate building and development. It was during these years that Rutstein was able to undertake building campaigns throughout Brooklyn, and especially in Brownsville, Brooklyn, and Crown Heights - small at first but increasingly larger over time. The New York Times would eventually describe Rutstein as "a pioneer builder in the Brownsville-East New York section of Brooklyn."

Milton Rothstein described Jacob's business ethic that led to this success. As Milton observed, Jacob "was the toughest businessman, never giving an inch. He would try to buy at zero and sell for a million... Whatever he did he was fabulously energetic despite the aftereffects of a rheumatic heart." "If he owned something it was worth a "million." If he wanted to buy something it was worth zero. He tried to get the last penny in selling and tried to buy as cheaply as possible." "He was heartless in his dealing with customers at times. He loaned vast numbers of small loans to building [owners] [and] in this way he always got the lumber sale."

---

[54] Other Rothsteins relatives in the United States were also in the lumber business. It may have been a profession of the family in Europe.

Nominal Measurements

Since 1918, J.R. had been experimenting with cutting lumber logs along with new nominal lumber measurements. Rutstein innovated an 11/4 wood plank (2 ¾") whereby the price of lumber was reduced 1/12 or about eight percent. At the time, most panels were a '2 by 4,' a beam of 2" x 4" that J.R. reduced to 2" x 3 ¾."[55] Rutstein, who was influential over large lumber fields and mills, spent over a decade convincing others in the industry to instead cut the beams 2 ¾' or 11/4 inches thick saving the ¼" thereby increasing efficiency by eight percent.

According to Milton Rothstein:

[Jacob] innovated an 11/4 plank whereby the price of lumber was reduced 1/12 or about 8%.... Most floor beams were 3/10th by 8/4th dressed four sides after going through a planer and the 8" or 10" wood 7 5/8 or 9 5/8" in width. J.R. got the mills to cut it 2 ¾" or 11/4 inches thick saving the ¼". This led to savings by increasing the yield of each cut on the log by an approximate 8%. It was hard to institute something new in an industry [with practices established and accepted over a period] of hundreds of years. Jacob persisted and finally this [innovation] was [adopted] on the West Coast and was called "Jew-Plank." ... But J.R.'s

---

[55] Milton also spoke about innovations regarding "3/10 x 8/4 dressed four sides after going through a planer and the 8" or 10" wood 7 5/8 or 9 5/8" in width."

innovation of "Jew-Plank" is still [used today] and [has been] a major [method used in the lumber industry] from 1918 on[wards.]

By 1930, Jacob was able to convince mills on the West Coast to adopt the standard and it was called colloquially "Jew Plank." According to Jim Denison, in the history of his lumber industry, Jacob "wanted this low-grade lumber to use for shoring, for five stories of basement, for parking lots, and a lot of those skyscrapers. So [people in the industry] called this Jew Plank that they cut, and it was a three-inch thickness, a rough cut, and put on ships. There was Calmar Lines that came into Newport from the Suez Canal route, getting out to the West Coast. They brought steel out from the East Coast and delivered steel and took lumber back to the East Coast again." This innovation would change the lumber industry and permanently adjust the structure of the lumber industry to J.R.'s nominal measurements into modern times. It also made Jacob millions.

Jacob as Charity Worker & Lumber Magnate

According to Helaine Blumenfeld, as soon as Jacob made any money, he began to give it away – first at home and then later in philanthropy. Jacob's lumber business and real estate holdings not only supported his wife and children. Jacob also employed his brothers, nephews, nieces, their spouses, cousins, and other individuals from Tolochin. Bessie Boyarin worked for Jacob Rutstein as a bookkeeper. Phyllis Birnbaum recalls that Jacob Rutstein's lumberyard owned many horses. The horses were used to deliver the lumber to building sites in the early days of the company. One day, when the horse driver didn't show up for work, Bessie Boyarin mounted the horses herself, directed the loading of the wagon, and drove the horses out of the lumber yard and delivered the lumber herself. It was while working for Jacob that Bessie met Mayer Markowitz, her future husband. Jacob gave a vast amount of small monetary gifts, grants, and interest free loans to his relatives, all of which helped jump start the success of his larger 'tribe' in America.

By the 1920s, history records the first major references to Jacob Rutstein as a philanthropist. Recalling the trauma surrounding his health and immigration to the United States, Jacob did what he could to ensure that other people would be able to receive affordable healthcare. On Sunday, July 19, 1925, the Brooklyn Daily Eagle reported that for "the first time in Brownsville community work, $60,000 has been raised by 20 men

START HOSPITAL DRIVE

5,000 New Supporting Members Sought for Beth El.

Jacob Rutstein, treasurer of Beth El Hospital, said that plans have been made to canvass synagogues in Brownsville and East New York during the High Holiday services in an effort to enroll 5,000 new members to support the hospital.

Rutstein said that never before in the history of the hospital has there been such demand for free treatment.

especially for Brownsville and East New York Hospital to be used for the Nurses Home and Training School." The article reports that the Chairman of the Building Committee, Jacob Rutstein, donated $5,000 [this is the equivalent of $75,000 in 2020 dollars]. Over the next few decades, according to Milton Rothstein, Jacob would every Sunday devote "his day to the hospital for years going to meetings there." During the work week, when he finished his work during, "he was there directing the contractor on the technical ends of the building operations.

Isaac Siegmeister, honorary secretary of the hospital, as toastmaster, lauded Jacob Rutstein, treasurer, who became ill shortly after his appointment as chairman of the dinner committee, but continued to work for the dinner's succes from his sickbed, which he left to attend the function. Siegmeister also praised Paul Polsky, who, as associate chairman, substituted for Rutstein, and Max DeKaye, superintendent of the hospital.

On July 13, 1927, the Brooklyn Daily Eagle reported the opening of a nurses training school. The article states, "Jacob Rutstein, chairman of the building committee, announced a $90,000 deficit was borne by the directors." The article continues that a "gold key to the building was auctioned to Jacob Rutstein for $7,000."

On December 10, 1928, Rita "Ricky" Rutstein, Jacob and Bessie's youngest child, was born in Brooklyn, New York. On June 26, 1932, the Brooklyn Daily Eagle had an article on "Brides of Interest." Among those discussed was Mrs. Abraham Becker. The article states that before her marriage, Mrs. Becker was Mrs. Bertha Rutstein, daughter of Mr. and Mrs. Jacob Rutstein of 1388 President's Ave. They are on a trip to Albany." The wedding was extravagant.

Prior to the depression, Jacob was reported to have been among the wealthiest Jews in Brooklyn. Even after the advent of the Great Depression, he remained a multi-millionaire and continued his charitable work uninterrupted.

While increasing his philanthropic activities in 1930, Jacob formed the Prudential Lumber Corporation. Despite the collapse of the global economy, demand for cheaper lumber increased not only in New York but nationally. Prudential Lumber Company was one of the most successful lumber companies in New York during the 1930s and 1940s. The company did business with Fred Trump, the father of President Donald Trump, and his family, as well as with the LeFrak family, also a major holder of New York State real estate. Jacob's daughter, Bertha, and her family would one day come to live on the same block as Fred Trump and his son, future President, Donald Trump. The families' children played together.

Beth El Hospital Seeks New Members to Aid Institution

Jacob Rutstein, treasurer of the Beth El Hospital, Rockaway Parkway and Avenue A, formerly known as the Brownsville and East New York Hospital, declared to-day that every synagogue in the Brownsville and East New York section will be canvassed during the High Holiday services in an effort to enroll 5,000 new members to support the hospital. In making this announcement, Mr. Rutstein declared:

"Never before in the history of the Beth El Hospital has there been such an increased demand for free treatment Our institution has been one of the greatest sufferers in the recent economic depression. According to our records the treatment of free and partly free cases has reached 91 per cent., a record for philanthropy in the history of the medical world. We are organizing a 'Flying Squad' of directors who will go from synagogue to synagogue, give the congregations facts and thus we are confident we shall reach our full quota in this emergency drive."

On February 23, 1933, the Brooklyn Daily Eagle announced that Jacob Rutstein was named to a committee at Beth El Hospital, formally known as Brownsville and East New York Hospital. On November 12, 1933, an article appears which contains a picture of Jacob Rutstein. The caption provides, "Jacob Rutstein, prominent charitable worker and treasurer of the Beth-El Hospital, is active in obtaining subscription reservations for the hospital's 10th annual dinner to be held at the Waldorf Astoria on Sunday evening, December 3. This annual dinner attracts an attendance of 1,200 and the proceeds go to the annual deficit."

DAILY EAGLE, NEW YORK, SUNDAY, NOVEMBER 4, 1934

UNITED TO REMOVE BETH EL HOSPITAL DEFICIT

An attendance of 1,500 persons at $50 a plate is the goal of the Beth El Hospital for their annual dinner at the Hotel Waldorf Astoria, Manhattan, on Dec. 9. The entire proceeds will go toward the $61,000 deficit. The dinner committee, left to right, Samuel Strausberg, treasurer; Meyer Kenin, secretary; Louis Plotner, chairman, and Louis Klein, vice chairman. Standing from left to right, Irving Altman, Jacob Rutstein, Joseph I. Aaron, president of the hospital; Harry Weinberg, vice president and Isaac Siegmeister.

A similar article and picture appear on December 13, 1934. On December 15, 1934, another article appears describing the opening of the Beth-El Hospital bazar and states that Jacob Rutstein was chairman of the bazaar committee and had helped procure $50,000 worth of merchandise which will go to the deficit of the hospital. A similar article regarding Beth El appears on November 1, 1937. Another article about an upcoming Beth El hospital dinner appears on May 5, 1940, representing every profession. The article cites Jacob Rutstein and states that Samuel Strausberg, acting president of the hospital, at a meeting of the dinner committee held last night, praised Mr. Rutstein for his untiring efforts in helping to make the dinner a huge success." Mr. Strausberg added that from "early morning until late at night, Mr. Rutstein and his committee are giving up their own businesses in an effort to obtain subscriptions for the dinner[56]."

During the Second World War, President Roosevelt asked Jacob Rutstein to sit on the War Standards Board for the commodification of lumber.

The last years of Jacob's life were spent nearly entirely on philanthropy. Bessie was, according to Ruth Paretzky Hershkovitz, a driving force behind Jacob's charitable giving. Jacob and Bessie separated themselves socially at times as they had something else to do – like charity functions and gala dinners. Helaine Blumenfeld relates that Jacob respected her charity work and often consulted her on matters of public service.

BROOKLYN DAILY EAGLE, NEW YORK, THURSDAY, NOVEMBER 22, 1938

News Page—Community Activities, Person

Arranging Dinner to Aid Beth-El Hospital

Milton Rothstein further describes some of Jacob's charitable work:

[Jacob] named [and founded] Pride of Judea, Brooklyn Jewish Center[57], Temple Petah Tikveh, The United Lubavitcher, where he devoted an enormous amount of work. Where there was a need for an executive, he was there. But much more, he schnored people in the streets for contributions (when he was in Miami, he solicited strangers and when he passed away had 45 checks in his pocketbook) for Beth-El [later Brookdale Hospital] and Yeshiva

---

[56] Another article for the same recurring annual Beth El event appears with Jacob's picture on May 21, 1940, May 7, 1941, April 21, 1942, May 30, 1943.

[57] Jacob was a founder of the Brooklyn Jewish Center and a friend of the cantor, Richard Tucker.

Chaim Berlin. In his later years, I would drive him to meeting after meeting every night except Friday and Saturday.

In or around 1940, Jacob was instrumental in bringing Rabbi Yosef Yitzchak Schneersohn, the sixth Lubavitcher rebbe, to the United States. Schneersohn, who was fleeing Nazi persecution, needed refuge in the United States. Jacob worked with other leaders of the Jewish community to help bring Rabbi Schneersohn to the United States. Once in the United States, Jacob is reported to have provided the initial infrastructure to Rabbi Schneersohn to launch Lubavitch in America. In addition to being the founder of the United Lubavitch Yeshivas, Jacob Rutstein helped Lubavitch locate and purchase the building which would become its headquarters in 770 Eastern Parkway. Jacob's son, Nathan Rothstein, an attorney, represented Lubavitch and did the closing of legal documents on the building. A picture of Jacob Rutstein hung in the Lubavitcher headquarters until the first half of the 1950's. According to Milton Rothstein, "when I was married, I had 200 or more Rabbis, including the son-in-law Rabbi Gourary of the Lubavitcher Rabbi Schneersohn" at my wedding.

On July 24, 1941, an article appeared announcing that "Miss Helene Jacobs is the daughter of Mr. and Mrs. Harry M. Jacobs … and the fiancé of Nathan Rothstein of 1388 President's Avenue." According to Ruth Paretzky Hershkovitz, Bessie had facilitated the introduction between her son and Ms. Jacobs. Bessie and the mother of Helene made the match after the two had

Jacob Rutstein. Brooklyn, New York, circa 1930s.

met at a charity function. According to Marjorie Rothstein and Helaine Blumenfeld, Nathan was a great Talmudic scholar and was going to be a Rabbi. He was the pride and joy of Jacob who was very happy when his children studied Talmud and engaged with the Jewish tradition. Nathan, however, changed his mind about being a Rabbi after going to Cornell University and Cornell Law School and became secular.

Jacob and his son Milton conflicted with one another over their different worldviews. Milton was very liberal, a 'fellow traveler' with socialist instincts. This contrasted with Jacob who was very conservative, a capitalist, and a Republican. According to Jay Rothstein, the roots of these differences began in childhood. Jacob was always working and was away for extended periods, which Milton resented and thus acted out as a child.

Jacob believed that Jews should follow tradition and that all Jews should have a formal Jewish education, which is why he supported Jewish schools. Towards that end, Jacob was a founder of the Chaim Berlin Yeshiva in the United States where his son Nathan would eventually attend. An article on March 16, 1942 states that "$2,000 was raised in outside gifts by Jacob Rutstein who recently returned from Florida." On December 11, 1944, an article appears in which it states that, "Yesivah Rabbi Chaim Berlin, one of the largest Orthodox Jewish institutions of learning in the country, is dedicating its new

BROOKLYN EAGLE,

Jacob Rutstein

Jews to Dedicate 7-Story School

Orthodox Jewry from all parts of the nation will join with Brooklynites in a week's observance of the dedication of the new seven-story building of Mesivta Rabbi Chaim Berlin, Jewish institution of learning to be held starting Dec. 10.

The school, which includes a secular high school and a rabbinical division, is at Stone and Pitkin Aves. According to Jacob Rutstein, dedication chairman, the building cost $1,000,000 and its upkeep will be approximately $250,000. More than 200 religious, fraternal, philanthropic and social groups have signified their intention of attending the exercises.

Abraham Meltzer is president of the institution and Rabbi Samuel H. Prero is executive director.

seven-story building at Stone and Pitkin Aves. at ceremonies which will take place throughout the week. The opening ceremonies were attended by more than 3000 persons. Jacob Rutstein, chairman of the dedication committee, announced that $25,000 had been donated by those present for the new $1,000,000 building."

Another article appears about Jacob and his work on December 29, 1944, stating the following:

"Our congratulations to Jacob Rutstein for his constant activity on organizing activities for the advancement of orthodox Jewish secular and religious education. Outstanding in his philanthropic activities is his recent purchase of the seven-story $1,000,000 building at 350 Stone Ave. for the Mesivtah and Yeshivah Rabbi Chaim Berlin in the hearts of Brownsville. Already, the institution has been recognized by the State Board of Regents through the granting of a charter and 800 students are now enrolled. Of this number, 150 are studying for the rabbinate. Also, 200 of its students have come from all parts of this country and 62 are refugees driven from their homelands by Hitler. This has been a truly humanitarian endeavor on the part of Mr. Rutstein."

On September 30, 1945, another article appeared with a photograph of Jacob Rutstein and a rabbi and local politician. The caption reads that "Jacob Rutstein, standing, will be honored at a dinner of the Brooklyn Talmudical School and Yeshivah Rabbi Mayer Berlin in the Hotel St. George on November 25 for his help to the institution."

TO FETE BENEFACTOR—Jacob Rutstein, standing, will be honored at a dinner of the Brooklyn Talmudical School and Yeshivah Rabbi Meyer Berlin in the Hotel St. George on Nov. 25 for his help to the institution. Co-chairmen of the dinner committee are former Investigations Commissioner William B. Herlands, left, and Morris Sukoff.

On November 26, 1945, an article appeared announcing a $350,000 expansion drive of the Chaim Berlin Yeshiva which commenced after the honoring of Jacob Rutstein "who helped purchase the school's $1,000,000 building." The drive was motivated, says the article, in part by the destruction of the leading schools of Jewish studies in Europe and the obligation of American Jewry to perpetuate the Yeshiva as the fortress of traditional Jewish religious education based on the Torah.

The Last Years

During his last years of life, Jacob spent time in Spring Valley, New York. He owned a large home on Passaic Road which was then situated in the countryside. His children and grandchildren would come to visit him and Bessie at the home in the summers. There he would sing old Jewish songs and sit in the shade as young cousins would play with one another. Helaine Blumenfeld recalls that Jacob would quiz her on subjects and that then reward her for the correct answers—something that triggered her inquisitive spirit. Jacob would also sing her Hebrew songs. Milton often recalled Jacob saying, "good swimmers drown, poor swimmers seldom ever" and that, "an ounce of honey can influence an enemy more than nine six-shooters."

Jacob Rutstein died on February 27, 1946 in Miami, Florida. The next day the following obituary appeared in the New York Times:

JACOB RUTSTEIN DIES AT 67: BUILDER, PHILANTHROPIST

Miami Fla., Feb 27—Jacob Rutstein, 67, a pioneer builder in the Brownsville-East New York section of Brooklyn and an outstanding philanthropist worker died of a heart attack here early today. With him when he died was his wife, Mrs. Bessie Rutstein.

Mr. Rutstein, who lives at 1388 President St. Brooklyn was in Miami in the interest of the Brooklyn Talmudical Academy, for which a $1,000,000 seven-story building on 350 Stone Ave. in that borough was recently purchased by him as chairman of the *institution's building committee. While here, he had interested a number of persons in giving substantial gifts to carry on its work.*

He was one of the founders of Beth-El Hospital, Brooklyn and a former treasurer of that institution. In his home borough, too, he was one of the founders of Temple Petah-Tikvah and the Crown Heights Yeshiva. He also was a member of the board of governors of the Brooklyn Jewish Center and took a vital interest in the activities of the Brooklyn Hebrew Home, the Home for the Aged, the Pride of Judea Home, and the Home for Incurables.

For many years, Mr. Rutstein was President of the Prudential Lumber Company, Brooklyn and many years ago took a leading part in the erection of apartments and other dwellings in Brownsville. Recently, he devoted particularly his entire time to philanthropic activities.

Surviving besides his wife are three daughters, Mrs. Bertha R. Becker, Mrs. Dora R. Bloom, and Rita Rutstein; a son Nathan, and five grandchildren.

Funeral service will be held Friday at the Brooklyn Talmudical Academy, with a number of leading Brooklyn rabbis participating.

A similar obituary was published in other newspapers, including the Brooklyn Eagle. Jacob's name continued to appear in the newspaper through 1950, the last being the announcement of the marriage of his daughter Rita on April 9, 1950. Jacob was also written about in an encyclopedia of entrepreneurs as follows:

Rutstein, Jacob, lumber merchant, philanthropist, Pres., founder, Prudential Lumber Corp., Brooklyn, N.Y. One of the founders of Beth-El Hosp., Mesivta Rabbi Chaim Berlin, Brown Heights Yeshiva, United Lubavitcher Yeshiva, Dir.: Brooklyn Home of the Aged, Home for Incurables, Pride of Judea Orphans Home, Crown Heights Yeshiva, Jewish Theological Seminary, Brooklyn

Jewish Center, Stone Ave. Talmud Torah Mem. Temple Petach Tikvah for more than 30 yrs. Contributor to most of the Yeshivas in U.S., Palestine and other countries. Veteran Zionist and long-time member of Mizrachi and other religious, philanthropic and national organizations. Mem. Miami Beach Jewish Center. Hobby, collecting funds for charitable institutions.

b. Tolochin, Russia, Apr. 1878, s. of Dov Ber and Rebecca: arr. in us., 1902; m. Bessie Poretzky; ch. Bertha (Mrs. Abraham Becker); Nathan, Dorah (Wife of Dr. Joseph Bloom); Milton, Rita; res. 1388 President St., Brooklyn, N.Y.; off. 769 Rockaway Ave., Brooklyn, N.Y.

Advertisements for his funeral were found in numerous newspapers such as these below:

JACOB RUTSTEIN DIES AT 67; BUILDER, PHILANTHROPIST

Miami, Fla., Feb. 27—Jacob Rutstein, 67, a pioneer builder in the Brownsville-East New York section of Brooklyn and an outstanding philanthropic worker, died of a heart attack here early today. With him when he died was his wife, Mrs. Bessie Rutstein.

Mr. Rutstein, who lived at 1388 President St., Brooklyn, was in Miami in the interests of the Brooklyn Talmudical Academy, for which a $1,000,000 seven-story building at 350 Stone Ave. in that borough, was recently purchased by him as chairman of the institution's building committee. While here he had interested a number of persons in giving substantial gifts to carry on its work.

He was one of the founders of Beth-El Hospital, Brooklyn, and a former treasurer of that institution. In his home borough, too, he was one of the founders of Temple Petach-Tikvah and the Crown Heights Yeshiva. He also was a member of the board of governors of the Brooklyn Jewish Center and took a vital interest in the activities of the Brooklyn Hebrew Home, the Home for the Aged, the Pride of Judea Home and the Home for Incurables.

For many years Mr. Rutstein was president of the Prudential Lumber Company, Brooklyn, and many years ago took a leading part in the erection of apartments and other dwellings in Brownsville. Recently he devoted practically his entire time to philanthropic activities.

Surviving besides his wife are three daughters, Mrs. Bertha R. Becker, Mrs. Dora R. Bloom and Rita Rutstein; a son, Nathan, and five grandchildren.

Funeral services will be held Friday at the Brooklyn Talmudical Academy, with a number of leading Brooklyn rabbis participating.

Final Services Tomorrow For J. Rutstein, Builder

Funeral services will be held tomorrow morning for Jacob Rutstein, 67, of No. 1388 President street, a builder in the Brownsville and East New York section and a leader for many years in Jewish philanthropies, who died yesterday of a heart attack in Miami. He had been in ill health for more than a year.

Mr. Rutstein was president of the Prudential Lumber Company at the time of his death. In 1938 he organized a building campaign to enlarge and improve the Mesita Rabbi Chiam Berlin, a Talmudic Academy. He was founder of the Beth-El Hospital, a member of the board of governors of the Brooklyn Jewish Center and a founder of the Pride of Judea Children's Home.

Tomorrow's services at 10 a. m. will be from the Mesivta Rabbi Chiam Berlin. Besides his widow, he leaves two sons, Nathan and Morris and three daughters, Mrs. Bertha R. Becker, Mrs. Dora R. Bloom and Miss Rita Rutstein.

At his funeral, the police closed off the streets. All kinds of people, from all kind of backgrounds—black, white, Jew, Christian, came out to pay their respects.

119

A letter written by a famous Rabbi, Nosson Telushkin, father of Rabbi Joseph Telushkin, memorializes Jacob as follows:

March 13, 1947

To the Wife and Children of the late beloved Mr. Jacob Rutstein:

I, who have had ample opportunity to witness the devoted efforts of your great husband and father for our Torah, for Judaism and for the welfare of our people, sick or well, wished to commemorate his wonderful work. I, therefore, wrote a few words in Hebrew with his initials forming the first letters of the lines, wherein I described his wonderful work for our people and Torah.

I wrote of his being one of the chief founders of Beth-El Hospital where tens of thousands of sick Jews have found their cure, of his great work for the cause of Torah in acquiring and building the Mesifta of Rabbi Chaim Berlin, to which cause he devoted his very heart and soul, and also of the whole-hearted cooperation he gave to the famous Rabbi of Lubawitz in erecting his great Torah institutions, United Lubovitcher Yeshivoth.

I also mentioned his devotion as husband and father, as friend, and his immense love for mankind. I spoke of the great love people had for him and of the esteem in which he was held.

I intended to write this or part thereof on his monument, but since this was not possible, I gave it to a scribe who wrote it on parchment. I then had it framed.

May his memory be blessed.

Sincerely yours, [signed] Nosson Telushkin

Brand 2-1623

ב"ה ניסן עלוישקין
RABBI N. TELUSHKIN
340 PENNSYLVANIA AVE.
BROOKLYN, N. Y.

March 15, 1947

To the Wife and Children of the late beloved
Mr. Jacob Rutstein:

I, who have had ample opportunity to witness
the devoted efforts of your great husband and
father for our Torah, for Judaism and for the welfare of our people, sick or well, wished to commemorate his wonderful work. I, therefore, wrote
a few words in Hebrew with his initials forming the
first letters of the lines, wherein I described his
wonderful work for our people and Torah.

I wrote of his being one of the chief founders
of Beth-El Hospital where tens of thousands of
sick Jews have found their cure, of his great work
for the cause of Torah in acquiring and building
the Mesifta of Rabbi Chaim Berlin, to which cause
he devoted his very heart and soul, and also of the
whole-hearted cooperation he gave to the famous
Rabbi of Lubawitz in erecting his great Torah institutions, United Lubovitcher Yeshiveth.

I also mentioned his devotion as husband and
father, as friend, and his immense love for mankind.
I spoke of the great love people had for him and
of the esteem in which he was held.

I intended to write this or part thereof on
his monument, but since this was not possible, I
gave it to a scribe who wrote it on parchment.
I then had it framed.

May his memory be blessed.

Sincerely yours,

Nissen Telushkin

121

According to Milton Rothstein, Jacob was a staunch republican and was anti–liberal. Jacob held out against the unions to the very end, fighting change, and reflection his ragged individualism. He would rather pay more to the men then have them gain the unions. According to Milton Rothstein:

> *[Jacob] never lavished or treated himself as a millionaire in later years. He shined his shoes nightly and bragged he could wear them ten years. In reverse, his suits seemed to last forever. He sported a walking cane and spat on his shoes. He meticulously hung his clothing on a hanger prior to going to bed. He would be clean shaved every day and with his blondish mustache looked the appearance of a well-dressed upper-class gentleman.*

Reflecting upon Jacob's life, Phyllis Birnbaum, a great niece of Jacob, remarked, "Jacob Rutstein was the American dream. That's how we came to America, because he was here. We always talked about him as the rich relative and he made it big in the Rutstein lumber yard[58]." In his family history, Milton's conclusion ring's true today, "I gave you insights to a man of distinction, a maven in the business world, a hero of the meek and oppressed, a defender of his faith, a Torah lover, and a genius for making money… There are few of us left who remember and recall his greatness. Perhaps you, with your gift of writing, will someday see fit to write of his blessed memory. Something will remain of one great person who has gone to the happy hunting ground of his ancient ancestors."

---

[58] She went on to say, "My father and my mother both worked for him; my father was the foreman and my mother was the bookkeeper and he helped take care of our family."

PART V

THE ART OF MATCHMAKING: AN INSIGHT INTO THE SHADCHANUT OF THE SHTETL

The Art of Matchmaking Shadchanut

The following 1902 letter was found within the Rutstein-Paretzkyn family archives. The letter contains many Yiddish proverbs and provides sociological insight into the activities of matchmakers and the culture of matchmaking in Europe during the 19th century. The letter captures the exchange between two matchmakers attempting to broker a marriage agreement between the daughter of a wealthy businessman, Tzvi Solevitchik of Humin, and an unknown party. Yiddish is typical of Belorussia and contains Russian, German, and Slovenian words.

It is unknown how the letter managed to find its way into the Rutstein-Paretzkyn family archives although it is possibly given to Jacob Rutstein as part of marriage negotiations between the Solevitchik family and himself. Assuming this is accurate, the marriage negotiations would fail as Jacob would ultimately marry Bessie Basha Paretzky, the daughter of Rabbi Tzvi Hirsch Paretzkyn and Esther Sarah Dubrow, in 1907.

Городъ Иошкенъ Тифлисской 10-го Июля
губ. Абраму Лейзеру Лейбову 1902 г.
Нишебургу ... № 11.

May 10, 1902
City of Igumen
Minsk Governorate
To Abraham Leiser-Leibov Nisnevich
for Sh. N.

בעסטער פריינד
שלומה גאלדין
אזוי ווא איך גיפין זיך יעצט אין

<u>איגומען</u> איז בייא מיר ארוף אויף
דעם זינען רחמנות האבין איבער א
מענטשין און ווער איז בילעבטער
דאס הויסט נעהענטער ווא איין
אייגענער מענש און אייך האלט אייך
פער איין אייגענעם מענשיין. דערום
זאלט איר זיין שטיל. און רויסט ניט
ווא א מיל.

און הערט צוא מיינע רייד מיט איין
גיפיל. נאר איר זאלט ניט לאכין. און
פון מיר חוזיק מאכין : וואס איך
קלער וועגין אזעלכע זאכין. וואָרום
איר קענט קלערין. ווא לאנג איך
בין אליין ארום גילאפין הערין : און
גיפאדעט ווא איין האן. און איך
האב ניט גערוואוסט וואס צוא טאן :
דערום ווייס איך אז עס איז שלעכט.
מיא ווארפט זיך נעבעך ווא איין
הערש. און קיינער פאר מיר דיא
<u>קאפיק</u> ניט ברעכט : נאר איך
אליינער האב זיך גיפונען

איין מענטשין פריינד. וואס עטליכע
רובל האב איך ניט פיינט און חוץ
אלץ איז דאס א גוטע זאך ווא מיר
שיינט : און איר דארפט פארשטיין
אזייא ווא איך בין אויף איין

To my Best friend Shloima Goldin:

Because I am now located in <u>Igumen,</u>
it came up in my mind to have pity on
a man who is beloved to me, closer
like a relative, and I consider you as a
relative. Therefore, you should now
conduct yourself in silence, and not
make noise like a windmill, and listen
with intent to my words. Do not
laugh or mock me—because you may
be thinking to yourself: Has it been a
long time that I myself was running
around [listening and] flapping my
wings like a hen? And I did not know
what to do or how to behave? I know
the meaning of suffering and difficulty.
We [matchmakers] are unfortunately
like a deer running around frantically
and nobody's heart aches for us. Only I
alone had discovered a friend to one
person, who is pleasing to other people
as who does not dislike a few rubles?

And in addition to that, this [what I
write] is a good deal/development as the

קאפיקע געבין גיוויין. און דאס האב
איך ניט גיצאלט וועט גאנצע _%_
קאפיקעס צאל גיין איז דאס
גיווײנליך ביליג שיין : איצט וועל
איך אייך אן הויבין צו

געבין בעטראכטען אלעס. איר זאלט
ניט מיינען אז דאס איז גירעט
באלעס : איר וויל אן הויבין שליסין
חתנים מיט כלהות : חתנים מיט
כלהות צו שליסין. איז דאס ניט
דיין גוטער ביסין קיין גוטער איד
זאל דערפון ניט וויסין : איידער מיא
הויבט אן צו געבין צו ערקלערין.
איז בייא איין אנדער כלה הויבט זיך
אן צו וויינזין טרערין און דאכט זיך
אז כלומערסט אז זיא וויל גאר ניט
הערין. חתן חתן הויבט זיא אן פון
רייד דעם שדכון צו שטערין. און
דאך וויל זיא וואס גיכער דיא ענדע
הערין : און איין אנדערע פון פרייד
וויים זיא גאר ניט וויא זאך
פארצואשטעלין נאר אזייא וויא איך
בין איין אלטער שדכון. איך וויים
שיין דיא נאטור פון יעדער מעדחען :
איז מיר

שיין גאר ניט שווער. צו ריידין מיט
א מיידיל וואס מער : דאס האב איך
גיגעבין צו פארשטיין. צו איין
כלה ריידין אז מען דארפן גיין : און
צו איין חתן אז מען דארף קומען.
די ערשטע זאך דארפט מען אנהויבין

truth shines and as it is supposed to be understood. Now you must understand, being that I was ready to give one Kopek, and that I did not receive of a whole any percent Kopeks be paid for the efforts of my labors, which are conveniently nicely considered cheap. But now I will begin to lift your spirits and allow you to think about everything. [But please] don't think that [what I write] is empty talk.

So, you want to bring together grooms and brides? To bring together grooms with brides is not an enviable task. May a good Jew never know from such a thing. Before you begin explaining the situation, tears might well up in the eyes of one bride. And it seems that she doesn't want to hear anything of "the groom, the groom." And she begins to interfere with the matchmaker with her conversations. And yet she still wants to hear soonest about the end of negotiations. Another bride may not even imagine her own happiness from her joy as she is so happy, she cannot describe it.

But because I am an old matchmaker, I know the full nature of any young woman. And to me it is not at all difficult. And yet to speak with a girl,

רייידין וועגן די מזומן : אין דערנאך
גייט ארויס דער חתן : און הויבט זיך

אן צוא בלאזין : און הויבט זיך אן
צוא פרעגין בייא שדכון וואס
דערווייל גיט ער איין א פאפיראס :
דער שדכון איז זיך דערפון צוא
פרידין. ווארום גיווייינליך אלע
שדכנים זיין ארעמע אידין : (אויף
מיר זאלט איר ניט חושד זיין איך
רייכין גאר ניט)
און צוא קויפין פאפעראסין דארף
מען דאך
האבין איין גראשין : און ער איז.....
און דער
ווייל מיינט ער אז דער שדכון איז
שיים _____

אזייא מיין פריינד פירט זיך דיא
וועלט. יעגעם איז גוט וער עס האט
געלד : און בייא וועמען געלד פאראן
וואס מער : צוא דערוף איז גוט זאל
זיין צוא זאמען איין פרויא מיט הער
און פערברייינגען זייער גוט און וואס
מער. און מיין בריף זאל אייך
זיין ניט צוא שווער : דיא גלאוונע
זאך איז

בעסטער פריינד שלומה אזוי וויא
איך ווייס שיים אייער מאן קען איך
אייך פארשטעלין איין פארשטיי עס
איז דא אין <u>האמין</u> איין שיינער
בה"ב צבי סאלאווועציק ער איז

this is what I have come to understand:
To one bride, we must speak to go;
and to one groom, that he must come.

The first thing we must begin talking
about [in any marriage negotiations] are
the available assets: and after that the
groom goes out: and starts to blow, and
begins to ask by the Shadchan, who in
the meantime, he gives a cigarette.
The Shadchan is excited by this
because it is so that all Shadchanim are
poor Jews. (Now, do not suspect this
of me, for I do not smoke at all and to
buy cigarettes you need to have a
Groshen: and I [have none]. In the
meantime, the groom thinks that the
Shadchan is already [satisfied].

This, my friend, is how the world
operates. The one who has money does
well, and those who have more of it, do
better. On top of that good [that money
brings the groom] shall there be
together with him a wife and they will
celebrate well. Now I hope that my
letter and its words should for you not
be considered too harsh.

My best friend Shlome, the fittest thing
is, being that I already know you are a
husband, I can present to you an
understanding [about a girl]. In the

זייער איין וואזנער מענטש אליין און
שטאמט אויך זייער שיין און דיא
פרויא זיינע שטאמט נאך שענער זיא
איז אליין פון

באברויסק זיא איז פון דיא
קאצענעלינסאנס
מיא קען זיך אויף אלס נאך פרעגין :
איז ביי זייא דאס הויסט בייא צבי
סאלאוועייציק פאראן איין טאכטער
זייער איין שיינע פריילוכן דאס
הויסט טאקע איין קראסאוויצע :
איר ווייסט דאך אז איך ווייס
וואס איין שיינער איז צוא דערוף
איז זיא זייער איין קלוגע און איין
גילערינטע אדנים סלאווארין איין

———————

1000 שדכון וואלט אייך שרייבין
נאר איך שרייב דיא ריכטעקייט
וויפיל מיא וועט לייגין צוא דיא
תנאים

איך האב דארטין גירעט האבין זייא
שיים נאך געפרעגט און זייא איז
אלס גיפעלין נאר מען דארף זיך
זעהען. דערום זאלט איר מיר תלמי
ענטפערין וויא קומט דאס אויס
ביי אייך. איך זאג אייך אז
דאס איז זייער גוט מאיר ניסנעוויץ

town of Humin, there is a very nice businessman named Tzvi Soloveichik. He is a very upstanding individual alone and also comes from a very nice lineage. And his wife comes from an even nicer lineage. She alone is from Bobruisk. She is one of those Katzenelsons and therefore one may even refrain from asking questions about everything regarding them.

By them, that is by Tzvi Soloveichik, there is a daughter a very pretty, happy one. This is one real uniquely special girl– a true beauty. You know that I know what beauty is. In addition, I know that she is very intelligent, well natured, and educated in several [languages]. Any other matchmaker would have written to you 1,000, but I write to you the truth about how much will be attached to the contractual agreement. I have spoken there, and they already asked questions and they liked everything they heard, and now we will only have to see what happens. Therefore, it is necessary that you write to me, about how it looks to you. I am telling you that this is very good [prospect].

Meir Nisnevich.

PART VI

RETURN TO TOLOCHIN SHTETL: A MODERN TRAVELOGUE

Summer 2005

Why go to Belarus?

I feel that in many ways my journey to Belarus, to the land of White Russia, was a century in the making. It seems natural to me that the land that nourished our ancestors for hundreds of years would somehow call out to at least one of its descendants. This calling found me, and it created a sense of curiosity and desire to re-explore a world that has almost vanished. Tolochin and Orsha were worlds that until very recently I could not adequately imagine, nor could I possibly comprehend. Until I began to explore my lineage, the story of my family, I knew scattered and incomplete details about that world from which my great-grandparents came and what their motivations were for leaving.

I knew only the following: My great-grandfather, Yaakov "Jacob" Rutstein was born in the small village of Tolochin, on April 15th, 1878. From looking at maps I could tell that Tolochin straddles the main road from Minsk leading to one of Belarus largest towns, Orsha. I knew that he was one of nearly a half dozen children born to Dov Ber and Riva Rutstein. As a child, I often heard stories about "Grandpa Jacob" and how he came to the United States in 1906, and within a decade made millions of dollars, going on to become the founder of dozens of Jewish institutions. As a child, Jacob took on mythological proportions which I mostly heard him referred to in the context of some Jewish institution or hospital or another which he helped found. But in the stories of Jacob, also known as Jay R, he had no personality, no desires, no dreams, hopes, or fears. He was just the millionaire immigrant ancestor, of which many of his children and grandchildren bore his name, including my father.

Bessie (daughter of Tzvi Hirsch) Poretsky Rutstein (1888-1947) and Jacob (son of Dov Behr) Rutstein (1878-1946), New York, circa 1909. Both were children of Tolochin.

I also knew two other pieces of information: First, that Jacob had five children, and they were Bertha, Dora, Nathan, Milton, my grandfather, and Rita - all of whom went their separate ways in life. Like the vast majority of American families, none of the descendants of Jacob are close to one another. Members of our small clan, especially of my generation, only meet at funerals, if at all. The second fact was that my great-grandmother, Bessie or Basha Poretsky, was also born in Tolochin and was a daughter of a Rabbi and great Torah scholar — Rabbi Tzvi Hirsch Poretsky. Bessie's voice, like many other woman's voices and narratives throughout history, were mostly lost.

It was with this scant information that I began my journey sometime six years ago. As a sophomore in high school, I remember feeling that by discovering my family roots and learning about my ancestors, I would somehow be paying homage to the people for whom I am a legacy.

Rabbi Tzvi Hirsch Poretzkyn (b.1857, d.1933) and wife Esther Dubrow Poretzkyn (b.1860, d. 1941) circa

As a member of the internet generation, I immediately began my search on the internet and found my way to www.jewishgen.org and joined the Belarus SIG mailing list as well as other groups on Jewishgen. I began to track down long lost relatives hoping that they could share their version of the family history to formulate a holistic picture of events and personalities. The representation that I was eventually able to create is, to a great extent, thanks to them.

Thanks to Jewishgen, I found two long lost cousins, also children of Tolochin, one from the Poretsky side of the family and one from the Rutstein side of my family – both of whom have been invaluable in my research. I want to thank my cousins Nancy Wexler (of the Rutstein family), for spending hours showing me around the New York City archives, and Gail Haymowitz (of the Poretzky family) for her loving support, guidance, and direction. The memoir of her journey to Tolochin can also be found on the Jewishgen website. Through the sharing of information, we were all able to fill the holes in one another's research and understanding of events. Thank you.

Preparing for the journey

After beginning my research, I was able to gather scores of disjointed facts, stories from various cousins, and artifacts such as pictures and old Yiddish letters. All this information became critical as it helped me reconstruct the larger family puzzle. I decided that I wanted to visit the shtetls from which my family came. I expressed the idea on the Belarus SIG and received many e-mails containing wonderful suggestions, tips, and experiences from others that have or have considered making the journey. One of the most important e-mail correspondences was from Yuri Dorn, the Coordinator of Jewish Research Group, and over the next year and a half, we corresponded about the possibility of my visit to Belarus. Yuri was great to correspond with; his knowledge and resources are vast and even extends to knowledge of the individual Jewish families that remain in the various towns and villages!

However, for various reasons, it was not viable for me to simply pick myself up and travel to Belarus to see the shtetls my family came from. So, months later, when I was accepted as a member of a student delegation to Ukraine, I decided that after my mission I would take this opportunity to visit Russia and Belarus since I was already in the "neighborhood." With several months' warning, I told Yuri the dates and he was able to reasonably secure me a letter of invitation to Belarus. The letter of invitation is necessary before any Belarusian embassy or consulate will grant someone a visa to enter Belarus. If it wasn't for that letter, I would have had to go through a travel company, many of which charge an additional fifty or sixty dollars just for the letter. After receiving the invitation letter, I sent my passport, letter of invitation, and flight itinerary to the Embassy of Belarus in Washington, DC. after dealing with the embassies of three Eastern European Countries that summer. I can tell you that my experience with the Embassy of Belarus was the easiest, (unlike Russia) the visa was reasonably priced, and the staff was friendly (as Eastern-Europeans bureaucrats go).

I want to point out that Yuri was even better able to help me with the logistics in Belarus because I knew what I wanted, and he helped me fill in the details. For example, I didn't want to hire a personal driver from Minsk to Orsha but rather to take the train. Why? First, because it's cheaper. But I also wanted to follow and live in the footsteps of my ancestors as much as possible, and I was certain that when they left Belarus, they didn't jump in their car and drive to Minsk to catch the next flight to New York. I also knew that I didn't need a guide as much as I needed a translator because I wanted to speak and interview as many people as possible in the shtetls I visited. Being specific, doing my homework, and having a game plan made it easier for everyone and helped me make the most of my time in Belarus. I would suggest that others do the same before traveling. Going to Belarus or anywhere else without a game plan can result in inefficient use of time and resources.

There are things that, in hindsight, I wish I had done but I didn't do. I wish I had brought more small gifts such as general Americana, and general medicine such as Tylenol or Advil. I also wish I had brought more cash and fewer traveler's checks. Additionally, and I have no real excuse for not doing this, I wish I had followed the advice of Marcia Loeb of California to write to the Mayor of Tolochin in advance. However, I didn't leave myself enough time to have the letter translated into Russian, and at the same time give the locals enough time to prepare. In an e-mail she sent to me on May 30 2004, Marcia Loeb writes, "Two years ago my brother and I visited Tolochin …It was an experience I will never forget! We wrote in advance (in Russian) to the Chairman of the town…we had a wonderful tour, and when we had finished, we were met on the steps by a delegation with flowers. In the delegation was the oldest Jewish citizen of the town…the mayor thanked us for coming and said, "Many people have left our little town, but you are the {only} ones who have ever come back." Referring to a Jewish family that hosted them she writes, "The warmth and love that was bestowed upon us that day will stay with us forever." I wish I had followed her smart advice but despite not doing so, I still had a tremendous adventure.

In addition, Shelly Dardashti of Tel-Aviv was able to direct me to a few key contacts within Belarus, one of them being Yuri Dorn. In turn, Yuri Dorn was able to give me many important details about the current state of Tolochin. In an email sent by Yuri Dorn on June 1, 2004, he states the following:

> "At present, 23 Jews live in Tolochin. Most of them are elderly people and live in mixed families. A functioning pre-war Jewish cemetery was preserved in the town. The location is to the left from the road from Tolochin to village Slobodka. Unfortunately, people began to make Christian burials at the cemetery. The building of a synagogue was not preserved — it was destroyed during the war. During the Holocaust in Tolochin, 2000 Jews were murdered. The place of execution is situated out of the town, not far from the village Raitsy. All the Jews were killed within a day on March 13, 1942. In 1960s, a memorial was erected at this place. The details of ghetto life and the facts of Jews execution one may find in the local museum at Pionerskaya ST., 4. The director is Pikulik Irina. The museum is located in the house that before the war, belonged to a rich Jew, who was an owner of a blowing shop. I believe it will be useful to visit this museum. I also believe

that meeting with people who can tell different facts about pre-war Jewish life in Tolochin probably will help you to gather necessary information."

I also went to local US archives and looked up ship manifests from Ellis Island, which sometimes contain former addresses, but at the very least contain important clues that blossomed once I arrived in Belarus. A lot of this can be done online and via snail mail. Also, as per the suggestions of the Jewishgen website, I brought old pictures, letters, and research documents which proved to be handy. I also familiarized myself on a basic level with the Cyrillic alphabet which later proved to be useful and is easy to learn.

Minsk, Belarus

I spent several weeks in Ukraine and Russia, witnessing the tremendous Jewish religious and cultural renaissance occurring in the Former Soviet Union, a renaissance of truly historical proportions. When I finally arrive in Belarus, I promised myself that I would come not just to seek out the dead but to learn and experience the living. Belarus is not just one big graveyard of the Jewish people. The Jewish people of Belarus are still alive! The descendants of our cousins who did not leave Belarus, those that stayed behind are still there — in the tens of thousands — and they need us. This renaissance that I observed could not have taken place and cannot continue to take place without the help of the world Jewish community. I implore those who honor and cherish the dead to give the same respect to the living. In Belarus, as in other places of the FSU, they need Jewish teachers, they need our love, our bodies, our knowledge, our donations — they need us.

I arrived on Sunday evening in Minsk from Moscow, and Leonid, the driver, was waiting (with a sign with my name on it) to pick me up at the airport. Leonid was very friendly and helpful. Yuri prepared all the logistics in advance. The driver took me back to the synagogue and religious community center where Yuri is the director and where I spent the night. The great thing about spending time at the center was that I was able to experience firsthand the renaissance of a religious Jewish life occurring in Minsk. The center has educational classes on Judaism for both adults and children, as well as a summer camp for local children. Months later, back in the United States, I met a girl named Yael or Tanya, a native of Minsk and a graduate of Yeshiva University, and who is now a student at law school at the University of Michigan. She told me that her first exposure to Judaism was at the summer camps managed by the Religious Jewish Communities of Belarus. She told me what an important role they have in reviving Jewish life.

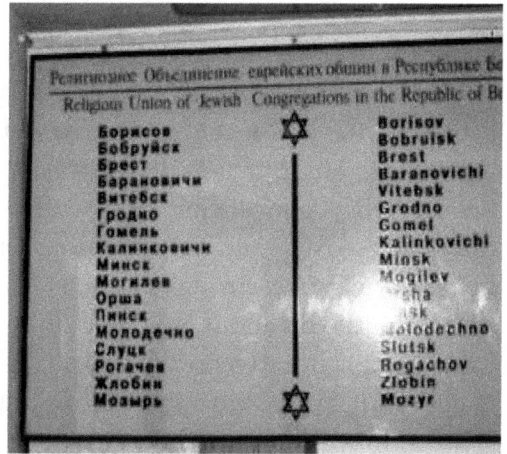

Some of the regions in which the Union of Religious Jewish Congregations operates in Belarus

At the center, there are daily prayer services in the adjacent synagogue and the center was able to provide me with kosher food. Everyone I met there was friendly and curious, and it was very meaningful to receive an *aliyah* during *shachris* while being in Minsk, Belarus! I also thought it's symbolic that on the day I arrived the *kehal* happened to daven *hallel* because of the *yomim noarim*. After *shachris,* I was escorted around the building by one of the local Yeshiva students. This center houses the only *Yeshiva* in Minsk and the closest thing Minsk has to a kosher restaurant. I also met a young man from Israel, just slightly older than myself. He had come to Minsk to volunteer for a year as part of a fellowship, a *shlichut*, in coordination with the Jewish Agency. I know from past experience that the Israeli government sends similar individuals to isolated Jewish communities around the world, including the United States. We spoke in Hebrew, but he was also fluent in Russian. He told me that his job was to run religious programming for the children at this center and to organize the youth for Jewish oriented events. It is educational programs like these that, in my opinion, will save what is left of the Byelorussian Jewry.

After breakfast, I finally met Yuri after having exchanged so many e-mails. He was friendly and compassionate, yet always to the point of business — just how I like things. Yuri escorted me back to his office from the dining hall to fill me in on the rest of the details of the trip, which he arranged on my behalf. His office wall was filled with photographs of great Belarusian Jewish leaders and Rabbis. It was through the pictures and maps on the wall that I first slowly became conscious of the fact that Byelorussian Jews were Litvaks and were strongly associated with the Lithuanian tradition. I also learned a little bit about Yuri as an individual. Yuri is a businessman and travels back and forth between Cleveland, where his family is, and Minsk. I could really intuit from being there how important the institution and its purpose were to him. Yuri mentioned that he and other Byelorussian Jews are trying to have the original Minsk synagogue restored to the Jewish community. The state now possesses the synagogue, which is now home to the national theater. I presume that the state seized the property during the soviet era. Soon my translator, a Jewish university student, arrived. Yuri informed Dmitry that he was to briefly show me around Minsk in the morning before the one o'clock train heading for Orsha arrived.

Dmitry, my translator and new friend, along with Leonid took me to two memorial sites for Jewish victims of the Nazi Holocaust.

If my memory serves me correctly, the site of this memorial was one of the places where the Jewish population of Minsk was massacred by the Nazis when they invaded and destroyed Minsk in 1942. During the war, this location was outside the city limits. The population forcibly marched outside the city until they were forced into the above ravine before being slaughtered. The statues below are symbolic of that crime. Dmitry also informed me that most citizens of Minsk are not aware of this memorial site, and that the general education about the holocaust is not a priority or on the agenda in Byelorussian society. It's not something that they "care about."

Memorial sites to victims of the Holocaust in Minsk, Belarus.

Dmitry and I were also taken to the local JDC building in Minsk. The JDC provides essential services all over Eastern Europe. Like the other JDC buildings I saw in Ukraine and Russia, this center provided medical attention to elderly Jews, family services, and childcare as well as other forms of social support. It had computer labs for students and was a conference and meeting center for various local Jewish groups. It was also the local headquarters for the JDC and their operations in Belarus. The JDC is World Jewry's best kept secret and really fulfills an important niche in Eastern-Europe. Additionally, as far as genealogists are concerned, the JDC building is also the location of the Jewish Museum in Minsk. The museum director is Dr. Inna Gerasimova who is an expert on the history of Byelorussian Jewry. I just happened to meet her while I was talking amongst some of the elderly, asking them where they were from, gathering some details, and exchanging formalities in Yiddish.

Inna was very excited to meet and speak with me. I gave her some information about my family history, which she will add to her database. For researchers hoping to learn more about their family history or about a town or region, she may be a good person to speak with. She has access to Yiddish papers and archives going back to the turn of the century. However, she does not speak English. One would only be able to communicate with her in Russian, Hebrew, or Yiddish. We spoke mostly in Hebrew,

The American Joint Distribution Committee center in Minsk, Belarus.

with Dmitry helping me when either of our knowledge of Hebrew failed us. She is currently working on various projects right now, including documenting Jewish participation in the general resistance movement and Jewish resistance to being murdered by the Nazis. She is trying to combat the myth that the Jews behaved passively during World War-Two and wants to publish a book for the general Byelorussian public but is unable to do so due to lack of funding. We decided that we would meet again in the late evening on Wednesday, the day before I left the country. She kept her word and days later, we met in the evening. She gave me a personal tour around the museum, and we arranged for an elderly Jew there to translate my Yiddish letters.

Engaged in conversation with Dr. Inna Gerasimova, I foolishly lost track of the time on early Monday morning. Her knowledge about the region, her ability to tell me tidbits of information about what was contained in my family letters, some a century old, captivated me. Dmitry kindly pointed out that we better leave soon, or else I am going to miss my one o'clock train to Orsha. Dmitry and I excused ourselves and promised to return another time.

We quickly grabbed our things. Leonid who was waiting seemed a bit apprehensive constantly saying that we weren't going to make it to the train and would have to catch the next one. I opened my wallet to get the money ready for the train when Dmitry pointed out that I had the wrong type of rubles. "Oy vey" was the only thought going through my mind. There was some conversation between the driver and Dmitry. It was suggested that we go find a place to change my dollars into Belarusian rubles and catch the next train. However, realizing that if we did that there was no way I could make my train, I insisted we try to make this one without having the proper currency. I was hoping (and I knew) in the back of my mind that somebody would take some of my US dollars.

We arrived at the train station and Dmitry tried to negotiate with one of the cashiers to accept US dollars, but she refused. Seeing the train pull into the station we started running towards the train with our bags bouncing over our shoulders. I was hoping that I could pay the more expensive fee by paying once we're on the train, like what they have in the United States. I asked Dmitry

At the Orsha train station. From Orsha to Minsk.

and he confirmed that there was such an option in Belarus. We successfully got on the train, put our bags down, and waited for the conductor. Many different thoughts were going through my head. Part of me wished I had taken Yuri's initial suggestion to use a private car from Minsk to Orsha. Or at the very least, I was thinking maybe I should have taken the first-class train instead of the "regular" train. Looking around the train compartments reminded me of some of the run-down New Jersey transit cars. There were people scattered at different ends of the cabin, each looking out into the abyss with angry looks on their face. I didn't feel scared or threatened by these looks because they were directed inward. However, I was just curious and confused. Why were people so angry?

I asked Dmitry why and I don't think I shall ever forget his answer. He told me that "people work really, really hard and they receive nothing in return...people are poor, and they are trying to figure out where their next meal will come from." As he spoke, the train conductor stumbled past us. "You see?" he said. "Look at her! She is drunk." He proceeded to tell me how someone like his mother, a university-educated woman, works two jobs just to make ends meet. Yet this uneducated, drunken conductor and his mother make the same salary. When I asked him about the political situation or why things were the way they were, he hushed me up. It was not something he wanted to talk about, and I gathered that it was because we were in a public place. I realized I had committed a significant fauxpas. In an unrelated topic of discussion, Dmitry also mentioned that because people are so poor, the conductors don't always check everyone's ticket out of compassion.

Throughout the early parts of the train ride, various conductors walked through the cabin until one finally stopped to ask us for our tickets. Dmitry explained to her that we only had dollars and not Byelorussian rubles. She said that we would have to ask some of the other passengers to exchange the money for us. Dmitry uncomfortably went to a few of the passengers to ask them, but nobody would touch the dollars because they thought they were counterfeit or that we were running some sort of scam. The conductor said she would come back later in the journey to collect our fare. I instinctively knew that the exchange between us was a charade. I knew that in the end she would accept our dollars. Echoing my thoughts, Dmitry told me that the only reason she didn't accept the money initially was because she thought that we were members of the secret police, the KGB. I sensed that she was thinking something along those lines from the way she looked at us, trying to size us up and our story. In the end, hours later, she did accept our dollars and her friend came in on the deal with her. They first spoke amongst themselves as to what would be an appropriate "deal." The conductor then told Dmitry that she wanted five dollars. My largest bill was ten dollars and so I just gave that to her. They looked at each other, then they looked at us stunned, as it was twice what they requested. Then, they quickly left the cabin all giddy with their booty. They didn't even give us any tickets. After they left, I asked Dmitry how much ten dollars was in terms of buying power and in proportion to daily wages. He told me that ten dollars were about two days' worth of wages. Putting myself in that situation wasn't probably the most intelligent thing to do, but it sure was an interesting experience.

At some point during the first half of the day, it came up in conversation that Dimitry did not know Hebrew, so I offered to teach him. It was on that train ride from Minsk to Orsha, from the 21st century to the 18th, that Dmitry and I sat together and learned the language of yore. We spent a large proportion of the train ride using my notebook as the means of learning about the Hebrew

An artificial lake in the Minsk City Center.

alphabet. Every time we would take a break from looking at our notebook and peek outside the train window, we were enveloped even more in rural territory. Minsk is a nice and charming city which seems to be developing nicely, but for every mile outside the limits of Minsk, one travels to less and less developed territory. The more outside of Minsk someone is, the less and less industry there is, the less phone polls, and less modern buildings. After spending some time talking and learning about Hebrew, we both peered out the train windows, slowly traveling to a different time and place.

Orsha, Belarus

We arrived in the early evening into the city center of Orsha after having crossed the Orsha River. The train station was one of the few buildings that were not destroyed by the Germans in both World Wars. It is a glimpse of the official architecture that existed during the turn of the century.

146

Waiting at the train station was Ilya "Yehuda" Halfey and Misha "Michael" Ginsberg who took me to the home of one of the members of the Jewish community of Orsha - Lazar and Tamara Tavger. I placed my things down in their home and then we went to one of the local markets where we purchased soviet style, some fruits, vegetables, milk,

The Orsha River at the turn of the 20th century.

and other miscellaneous stuff that I could find to suit my dietary needs. We went back to their home and sat together, talking, while eating dinner. Lazar and Tamara were generous enough to open up their home to other members of the local Jewish community in Belarus and allow them to use the home as a "community center" where people can conduct some sort of religious services and gather socially.

Ilya related some of the oral histories he had received from his grandfather about how life once was in Orsha. Orsha was once a very small town but grew to be a major center of Jewish life over time. Orsha was a well-traveled transportation center with major connecting points for trade and commerce. All this contributed to Orsha being a cultural center. In 1944, the railroad reached its peak of development which improved the life of the town. There were Jewish schools, and people from nearby towns would come to study at

Near the Orsha train station at the turn of the 20th century.

them. Orsha was the "place to be" and was mostly Jewish. It remained a vibrant Jewish center until it was destroyed by the Nazis in the Holocaust. Ilya related that he had a strong Jewish upbringing and that he never heard a word of Russian until the age of fourteen because he lived with his grandparents who only spoke Yiddish. He eventually learned

Ilya "Yehuda " Halfey and Misha "Michael" Ginsberg at the Orsha train- station.

Russian in school where he often got in trouble because he would write in Yiddish. Only recently did he start to relearn the religion that he said was taken from him.

At some point in the evening, we went to the home of a certain Boris, one of the oldest members of the Jewish community in Orsha[59]. I told him

The home of Lazar and Tamara Tavger and the Religious center in Orsha, Belarus.

who I was, why I had come from the United States, and that I was related to various families that had lived in Orsha before the war. He recognized the surname name of one the families: the Epsteins. From talking with him and with the other members of the Jewish community, I am of the impression that the Epstein family was a large clan or tribe amongst the Jewish community in

---

[59] I must mention that some of my notes were damaged and that I am not able to one-hundred percent confirm whether the following autobiographical statements contained in the immediate following interview are that of this same Boris that secretly baked matzah in his home or of the other Boris I interview later in this piece. However, I am about eighty-percent certain that the Boris I interview later is Boris Reitsen and that I never wrote down the surname of the Boris mentioned in the immediately following interview the one who secretly baked matzos. I have two different dates of births for the two different Boris's one is 1937 and the other is 1930.

the region and that the vast majority of them have moved to Israel in the last fifteen years.

Boris spoke of life in the city before the Second World War. Orsha was a center of Jewish culture. It contained two Jewish theaters and a tremendous number of Jews. There were four primary synagogues. The founder of the Lubavitch Chasidic movement, Shenur Zalman of Liady, lived not more than thirty kilometers from the city. Thus, there was some Chasidic influence in the city. Boris says that before the wars, people decided on which synagogue they would attend based on class and their professions. Boris says there were three children in his family, and the family worked in the tiles business. His family "was taken to war, fighting," and his father was in the army.

Before the Russian Revolution, Jews had the worst of jobs working for the lowest wages and in the most demeaning positions. Boris recalls that his mother and father would go to synagogue, but they didn't pray at synagogue. They "just went to go." However, everyone celebrated all the holidays and it was a big thing to do in town as everyone came together. Boris recalls that before the Second World War, Jewish and non-Jewish kids played together, and anti-Semitism was minimal. His mother didn't work, and his father worked with roof tiles and metals. After the war, there was a great demand for someone proficient in metal and roof making. Thus, business was good for someone like his father. Boris's father worked with the highest-quality metals, including those that are used in a kitchen such as metals for cooking and for pots. Boris's grandparents worked in a small (home) factory which was a family business. Children were all working full time by the age of sixteen. All or most of the shops in Orsha were owned by Jews and they dominated the metal-working industry and manufacturing. The Jews of Orsha were the primary advocates of culture and arts in the town.

The great pogroms of 1914, which occurred before the revolution, were mostly concentrated in the small towns around Orsha. There were big pogroms in all the small shtetls, such as Tolochin, and there was fear that the pogroms would spread from village to village. There were cases in which Jews protected their property and organized themselves into self-defense groups. Boris posits that things were easier for Jews in the smaller towns than in the larger ones, such as Orsha, as many of the smaller contained mostly Jews. Boris recalls a story that he heard of when some of the local peasants got drunk and started harassing and attacking Jews. One of the strong Jews, a gibbur, came out {presumably to defend himself or other Jews} and killed one of the non-Jews by punching him. Subsequently, in fear of retaliation towards this gibbur, the entire Jewish community united and gathered money from all the Jewish members of the town until there was enough money to send this gibbur to America.

During the cold war, it was forbidden for Jews to practice their religion. However, members of the community still wanted to observe the Jewish holidays, especially the Passover. Many others were still afraid because if they were caught celebrating Judaism, the police would arrest them and take them away. Boris and his brother, who now lives in Israel, risked their lives to bake matzot during this time period. Boris and his brother would secretly bake matzot while someone watched out for police, spies, or if anyone suspicious may be approaching his home.

This is the matzah machine that Boris and his brother used to make matazot secretly during the Soviet Era. The matza machine is now located in the Jewish Museum in Minsk and is under the care of Dr. Inna Gerasimova.

After we left Boris's home, we didn't really do anything else that evening. We did briefly visit the cemetery, but we decided to leave a more comprehensive visit for the morning. I was told that it isn't safe to travel, even for Byelorussians, around Orsha in the evening. So instead, Dmitry and I spent the evening indoors, read, learned some more Hebrew, and got to know one another.

The two pictures above represent the location where Boris and his brother baked matzot in secret.

I woke up early the next morning, the 6th of September, just towards the end of the sunrise. There was this misty, cool, and fresh feeling to the air which I haven't experienced before. There was no heating in the home, and I had only my covers to keep me warm from the chilly Byelorussian night. Waking up in such a home and walking out into the backyard with an open field, breathing the fresh air, and heading towards the outhouse was a very surreal experience. It allowed me to place myself in the shoes of those that left this land a century ago. It triggered my imagination and it made me intimately aware of the living conditions in which they likely lived. During the night, there were no lights when I went to use the restroom. I had to use my palm pilot light to direct me to where I need to go. I think it's hard for people in our society to imagine not having a light at night and the kind of feelings that brings. I am so glad that I didn't stay in the local hotel.

I understand from discussions with people that indoor plumbing is still rare. In the last few decades, people have begun running pipes from the main water network towards their property to have running water. Prior to that, people had their private wells that they used for water. Presumably, one would use this running water from a well or from the pipes outside their homes to cook and to draw a bath. The yard also contained a large backyard, a fallow field, and what looked like some fruit trees. I got the impression that the backyard of the home was more or less representative of other homes in the area. However, I would say that this property seemed to be on the larger side.

Top: a washing station, a place for winter wood storage and perhaps what is a workhouse; bottom: The inside and outside of the outhouse that we used.

Left: a stand filled with what looks like squash near the garden in the backyard; right: a large field which appears to be fallow.

After eating breakfast, we walked to the local cemetery which wasn't very far from where I was staying. The cemetery is located on top of a hill, which historically made it very difficult to bury people during the winter months when there was heavy snow. I was told that the Byelorussian government, beginning from Soviet times all way through the present, has had a bad habit of building on top of, and/or destroying Jewish cemeteries. The Orsha cemetery is one of the selected Jewish cemeteries that haven't been built upon or destroyed. That is because, over the years, it has become a mixed cemetery with Jews and non-Jews buried there. Destroying the cemetery would create tremendous opposition amongst the non-Jewish members of the city. However, the cemetery was originally only Jewish.

A Randomly chosen grave site in the Orsha Jewish cemetery. The tomb stone reads "An old man, simple and straight {with G-d} — Chaim Yitzchok the son of Tzion PATZARSKI

I took some random photographs of grave sites because I knew they would be of some interest to some other researchers. Most of the tombstones that date before the second war have been destroyed by man and nature, but mostly by man. However, there are a handful of tombstones that weren't destroyed by the Nazis or by local vandals that date before the revolution. Most of these tombstones are faded which makes it very hard to see what is written on them. One can see the remains of tombstones that jut out of the ground several inches.

Towards the back of the cemetery, there is tall grass that has grown on top of many of the grave sites. There are tombstones buried amongst the thick shrubs. In some of the newer sections of the cemetery, one can see the introduction of non-Jewish burial sites. On the outskirts of the cemetery, there are some shepherds and shepherdesses who graze their cattle. I wouldn't be

Two Jewish gravesites, one partially destroyed, which date from before the Russian Revolution.

153

surprised if occasionally some of their flock wandered off and entered the cemetery to graze. There seems to be no clear designation of the grazing area of where the cemetery begins or ends. This is mostly true in the most northeastern part of the cemetery.

A shepherdess along with her flock grazing on the border of the Orsha Jewish cemetery.

Belarus and indeed much of Eastern Europe are filled with things that may appear unusual to many Westerners. However, one thing which reminded me that I was in Eastern Europe, just in case I forgot, is the following story which I was told about the below grave. Orsha is known as a center of organized crime and several years ago one of the major mob bosses was assassinated. Though he was not Jewish, he was buried in the Jewish cemetery in the following grave plot.

A memorial to victims of the Nazi-Fascists at the back of the Orsha cemetery. This memorial, like many others in Belarus, does not mention that the primary victims of the Nazis were Jews. Some locals feel that Belarus has not done enough to educate its population about the unique Jewish experience in the tragedy of the Nazi Holocaust.

Grave site of a former Orsha mob boss in the Jewish cemetery of Orsha.

However, after he was buried there, people would come to his grave site and desecrate his tombstone. Sometimes they would unbury his grave and leave his body out in the open. So, in order to prevent this, the family built a booth directly across from his grave. The booth is capable of housing a full-time security guard in order to protect the grave site of this mob boss from vandals.

After we finished visiting the cemetery, we went to the JDC offices in Orsha. What was special about this JDC center was that it seemed to have a strong institutional framework, strong social bonds, and at the same time, it managed to create the feeling that this was a second home for many of its constituents. It had a very homey feeling to it. The Union of religious Communities in Minsk also had this feeling.

The security booth which is home to a security officer hired to protect the grave site of one of Orsha's former mob bosses.

Inside, there was a small crowd of people trying on clothing. The JDC had recently sent a shipment of mostly new clothes to the local members of the community. People were happily trying some of them on, some suggesting clothing to their friends and replacing some of their old tattered clothing. One of the people that I met at the center was said to be very knowledgeable about the history of Jews in Orsha. His name was Boris "Baruch" Reitsen. Boris and

I went outside to the backyard where I interviewed him. We would have spoken longer but we needed enough time to drive out to Tolochin.

Boris told me that the town of Dubrovna, northeast of Orsha, was a huge Hasidic capital and that part of his family was from that town. He told me that his grandfather paved roads for a living. His father worked in Dubrovna in one of the early factories that came to the region. As a child, he recalls hearing that there were pogroms and they frequently occurred until the 1930s. He said there was a beautiful stone tree monument/tombstone in the cemetery which dates to the time of one of the early pogroms from the time of the revolution. During the pogroms, some of the non-Jews would help certain Jewish families by hiding them. However, they were often tattled on by other non-Jewish families, and the hidden Jews would then be discovered and subsequently killed. I believe that this is the tombstone to which Boris was referring.

A monument or tombstone located in the Orsha Jewish cemetery possibly dating to the time of one of the great pogroms from the beginning of the 20th century.

The monument above is in memory of an entire family (or all the children of a family) that perished in these pogroms. If you focus on the above photograph, you can see the names of various people of one family; all appear murdered in the pogroms. These pogroms from the turn of the century and through the revolution contributed to Jewish emigration to the West. Boris conveyed how the days leading up the revolution, people were disappointed and disenfranchised with the Russian Empire, especially the Jews. In the

Jewish community, there was a large gap between rich and poor. Sometimes the poor Jews would steal or raid from the rich Jews. The poor Jews were angry and alienated from the Jewish establishment and were not satisfied with their lot. Boris believes that poor Jews would often complain to poor non-Jews about the rich Jews. Boris thinks that it could have influenced some of the poor non-Jews to engage in raids on Jews as a whole. However, unlike the non-Jews, Jews would never murder or commit violence against one another. Boris says that there were "middle class" Jews, but that just meant making enough to have the most "basic of necessities." The "middle class" in Orsha standards would probably be considered way below the poverty line in the United States. I posit that the middle class in places like Orsha at the turn of the century meant that the family was not starving and maybe had a few rubles saved up for emergencies.

Boris Reitsen at the JDC center in Orsha, Belarus.

Boris told me that his uncles were in the Russian army and that his Aunts went to study in Minsk. One of his aunts eventually died in the (German?) bombings of Minsk. Boris told me that he never went to *cheder* or any Jewish school but that two of his brothers did before the war[60].

During the Second World War, Boris and his family left Orsha and fled to Siberia. When he returned to Orsha, the town was absolutely destroyed by the fascists (Nazis). He lived in a barn until he was able to rebuild his life. The remaining Jews worked very hard to improve their lot, but they could

---

[60] In the Orsha Jewish school his brothers learned Yiddish as a language and that's mostly what made it Jewish.

not get ahead because they were Jews. It was true, especially when it came to university. As a result, many Jews changed their nationalities on their passport and their surnames so that they could get ahead in life. That is why, today, official estimates of the Jewish populations in Belarus are much lower than the actual Jewish population. Physical conditions did improve slightly after the war with the massive introduction of electricity. Cars also started to appear in the region, and running water replaced the personal wells which most people used.

Like before the war, people were afraid to announce that they were Jews. They lived their Jewish lives discretely, even after the war. There were lots of bickering and fighting in the Jewish community like before the war. "Two Jews, three opinions" Boris said chuckling. People were afraid to celebrate their Jewish identity in Orsha though many of them continued to observe Jewish holidays, mitzvoth, and other rites. Boris stated that everyone was proud of the secret baking of matzah which occurred during the Soviet era.

Dmitry standing outside what I have dubbed the 'shtetel mobile'. We used this car to drive around Orsha and from Orsha to Tolochin.

Tolochin, Mogilev Guberniya, Belarus

On the way to Tolochin, Ilya Halfey began relating the stories he knew about Tolochin. According to Ilya, during the "early" pogroms, people would run away from the village and hide in the forests. During the First World War, most of the pogroms were committed by Polish and Czechoslovakians. Pogroms up until 1917 were mostly committed by the Polish. Jews were often harassed, and it wasn't uncommon that a Jew with a beard or payis would be attacked and have his beard or payis cut off. Ilya's great-grandfather had his beard cut off by the Polish and Ilya recalls how humiliating that was for him. During the First World War, most of the pogroms against the Jews were committed by various Slavic groups — not by Germans.

The coat of arms of Tolochin located in the town center

I had also heard many stories about the pogroms and about the life in Tolochin from my various relatives. My cousin Ruth Poretsky Hershkowitz recalls her father, Aaron (Harry) Poretsky (1890-1972), speaking about some of his early memories. Aaron spoke of the time as a child when he was playing with his friends in the fields. When he returned to town, he saw the synagogue had been attacked and burned to the ground. It was this experience that encouraged him to become a Zionist. Historically, when the Cossacks attacked the Jews, the Poretsky boys would hide the girls in barrels of apples and potatoes to hide them from the Russian soldiers. Then they put the potatoes and apples on top of the girls to protect them. Rabbi Tzvi Hirsch Poretskyn had a sister named Basha who was married to Joseph Epstein that lived in Orsha. Basha had a friendly Christian neighbor which would hide her and her family during the pogroms. From the perspective of many Jews, pogroms were occurring all the time. In eighteen ninety-seven, a few years before the great migrations, there were about fifteen hundred Jews in Tolochin.

By the First World War, all the sons of Tzvi Hirsch Poretsky, my great-great-grandfather, had already left Tolochin and were working in the United States. The Poretsky boys had left behind their three youngest sisters. During the First World War, the Germans had come to Tolochin and treated the population relatively well. However, with the end of the First World War and the eruption of the Russian revolution, the situation deteriorated, and the locals started raping and pillaging Jewish targets in Tolochin and nearby villages. During the revolution, the Poretsky girls hid behind a long carpet that was hanging on the wall to avoid being raped in the ensuing pogroms. Then the Poretsky girls were forced to move from house to house and village to village to escape the raids and attacks. Simultaneously, in the United States, the Poretsky brothers frantically searched for their sisters but had difficulty finding them. They asked the American Red Cross to intervene and eventually the girls were found. The Red Cross eventually found the three girls and the brother's brought them and their parents to America on first class tickets.

In Tolochin, Tzvi Hirsch and Esther ran a local inn which people stopped at while traveling. They also owned a seltzer machine from which the family made most of its money. Owning a seltzer machine was a very big deal during this era. The family also had some sort of small farm with animals that needed to be released during a pogrom when the barn was set afire. Rabbi Poretsky also worked as a wheat broker. When Rabbi Tzvi Hirsch Poretsky arrived in the United States, he brought a whole box filled with rubbles with him. He was convinced that the Czar would return to power and that the money would become valuable.

A field outside of Tolochin and Kokhanova

160

According to Dr. Sylvia Sussman, people would come to ask him advice on Halachic issues as he received rabbinical ordination (*smicha*). He was an avid writer and continued that activity for the Yiddish TUG newspaper upon his arrival in the United States.

According to Ilya, Tolochin was once famous for its kosher meat and beef. It was good tasting and very cheap. Many Jews, including his grandmother, traveled to Tolochin from Orsha to purchase meat. Young men, *Yeshiva Bachurim,* would first travel to Orsha and then go over to study in Yeshivas like Mir, Volozhin and Vilna. Education was greatly desired amongst the Jews in the region. Only some could read or write "but all knew how to count money. If someone had a family of ten children, there would usually be at least one that could read and write." Ilya continued to impart stories to me as we trekked through the countryside on our way to Tolochin.

A *highway sign indicating the direction towards Tolochin.*

The road from Orsha to Tolochin is unbelievable. Imagine that you are in Belarus, in the beautiful hilly countryside. There are vast meadows filled with beautiful flowers and dirt roads. As you travel down one of these dirt roads, you see Belarusian peasants tending to their flocks and using oxen to plow their fields. Occasionally, you see a horse and carriage pull past you in the opposite direction. You approach a small village, a shtetl, the one your ancestors came from a century ago. The region has barely changed.

Upon arriving in Tolochin, we went to pick up Tamara Abramovna Kahovich, who was somehow a relative of the Lipshitz family, where we were going to have lunch. We also drove through the center of town and what I observed reminded me of Gail Haymowitz's description of people in Minsk, "All over the first impression is of people walking everywhere carrying fabric

161

shopping bags. No matter if they are young or old, male or female all carry these bags."

We finally arrived at the home of the Lipshitz family. I don't have the words to describe the warmth and the hospitality which was showered upon me by this family. They didn't have much but the little they had, they offered entirely to me. Their generosity towards a stranger made me realize that despite our material abundance in the United States we have not learned to be as generous as we could be.

Two Byelorussians traveling with a horse and "carriage" near the outskirts of Tolochin

Leonid Lifshitz was born in 1928, in Tolochin, Belarus. He is the son of Bracha Furhman and Yishiya Lifshitz. Leonid's grandfather was Eydola "Adolph" Lifshitz. According to Leonid, his family has lived in Tolochin for centuries, but today, he is the only one left. There are only a few Jewish families left in Tolochin, "everyone else went away," and nobody left speaks Yiddish or Hebrew. Leonid's family, like many others, was extremely poor before the war. There were some rich people in Tolochin, and they were mostly merchants. Poor people were those who engaged in an occupation like fixing shoes "or even worst working in forms of manual labor."

Two of the last Jews of Tolochin, Belarus: Mr. Leonid and Mrs. (Tamara?) Lifshitz

Leonid went to work at the age of twelve in the fields and the transportation of bread. "Nobody thanked me. I worked really hard and nobody thanked me, and I got nothing in return — nothing." People would call Leonid 'Zhid' which is a

162

derogatory word for a Jew. They would say the famous Russian maxim, "bey Zhidov spacie Racieu" which means "Beat (up the) Zhids and save Russia." For several minutes, Leonid complained that his entire life he has worked hard but has received nothing in return. He had two surgeries and has constant pain in his stomach. At this point in the conversation, everyone started talking at once and had a different opinion of how life really was[61].

The police station in the village of Tolochin. This building was once the location of the town cheder, where Jewish children were educated. I was told that this cheder and building was the same one used by the Jewish community prior to World War One and the Russian Revolution. That means this building may very well be the building where my great-grandfather attended cheder as a child.

---

[61] "14, 15, 16,17 — then ghetto during the war."

Leonid went to cheder for three years. There was only one school in town, but it was eventually closed because of socialism. According to Leonid, there were four synagogues in Tolochin. People would pray in the synagogue and wrap themselves in Teffilin. As a child, he would pray *Shachris, Mincha,* and *Maariv.* Everyone went to shul on Rosh Hashana and tried to kiss the Torah.

Leonid had relatives who fled to America. In order to leave the country, they needed a special guide to bring them to the border because Jews would never travel by themselves as they were not allowed to leave the country. Those who left were those that had some money. The really poor Jews could not leave. When someone wanted to leave, they would first get to the border and then have the special guide lead them through the dangerous forest towards Polish territory. Once in Poland, they would try to get to a port city such as Libau. They never had the problem of leaving behind possessions because most Jews had nothing to take. Most Jews ran away but the really sick and poor were not able to leave.

Leonid emphasizes how everyone in Tolochin was really poor. He recalls how his grandparents, the patriarchs of his family, had only dirty and worn-out clothing. Everyone thought about where their next piece of bread would come. Yet to a certain extent, it was good to be Jewish because Jewish people always helped one another.

An old home in Tolochin.

In 1935 and 1936, when Leonid was a young boy, there was a devastating famine in the region. The Byelorussian people were brought to their knees because of the famine. Leonid remembers people dying in the streets, and even more people died in the famine than in the pogroms. People ate dead bodies while the Russian government sent bread to Germany. The government sent bread to Germany up until the German sneak attack in 1941.

During the war, Leonid's uncle was killed by the Nazis. When the Nazi's entered Tolochin, they told all the Jews to move to a central location, then they divided Jews and non-Jews. They lined up all the Jews and gypsies into a straight line. The Nazis told all the Jews to step forward. However, Leonid's uncle looked Georgian and he didn't step forward. A Russian neighbor then asked one of the German soldiers why his neighbor, Leonid's uncle, had not stepped forward. Discovering his uncles' Jewish identity, the Nazis subsequently shot his uncle. In the ghetto, many were shot, killed, and raped by their neighbors. The phenomena of non-Jewish neighbors turning on their Jewish neighbors occurred everywhere. The remaining Jews, nearly two thousand, were then taken to the ghetto in Kohanisk. While many of the Jews were shot in the town, most were brought by carriage to Raitsy. The Nazis used Crimean's to assist them. In Raitsy, the Nazis stripped the remaining Jews of their clothing and marched them to what would be their common grave on the outskirts of town.

The road used on the Nazi death march. This road leads towards the mass grave near Raitsy.

Leonid walked to Borisov where his uncle had a horse. Then, they rode through the forest observing the tanks, the bombings, and soldiers killing people. They rode on horseback as far as the town of Kogan. At some point, Leonid boarded a train heading east. On the train ride, he heard a man talking about how he wanted to kill all the Jews and communists and couldn't wait to do it. At that moment, a bullet coming from outside the train went through the window into this man's head and his brains exploded all over the place[62]. After spending the rest of the war in the east, Leonid returned to Tolochin in 1946 only to face famine and hardship in rebuilding his life.

When Leonid was a child, he had difficulty seeing, and his mother would always tell him to go to Epstein who was the eye doctor. Before the war, Tolochin was a classic shtetl. But after the war, it became a town. As a child, he heard lots of stories about strong and big Jews that saved the day. Leonid had a relative that picked up a horse on his shoulders. Nearly sixty percent of the town was Jewish, and it seemed as if Jews were everywhere. His mother would always cook before Shabbas. They were very poor growing up, but they had their best food on Shabbas even though there wasn't much food. When people got together, they always spoke about wanting to marry off this guy with this girl and this girl with that guy. There were three or four synagogues in Tolochin and all believed in G-d before the war. Unlike in Orsha, people just went to the closest synagogue. There was a huge wood industry that has all products related to wood such as carriages and homebuilding. A lot of people made their income through something related to lumber. His Lifshitz's were carriage drivers★.

I learned that the Lipshitz family knew some members of the Rutstein clan who lived in Tolochin. It turns out these Rutstein are distant cousins of mine who never left town. The last of the Rutstein clan eventually moved out of Tolochin and now reside in Beersheva, Israel. Later that day, I found a tombstone with my surname at the Tolochin cemetery.

Later on, we left the Lifshitz home and Leonid accompanied us to the location where the Jewish population of Tolochin was murdered by the Nazis. We drove outside of town towards the mass grave to pay our respects to the dead. A large mound jutted out of what was surrounded by flat earth.

---

[62] He had a brother that lived from 1925-1943 whom died in the war.
★See below for other interviews conducted at the Lifshitz home.

While it may not be clear from the photographs, the area where the Jews were executed was near the family homes that existed at the time of the Second World War. It would have been impossible for anyone not to have noticed the Jews marching through the area. The ensuing gunshots would have been heard very loudly and clearly by the locals.

Leonid at the mass grave where the Jews of Tolochin were massacred.

Ilya removed his prayer book and began to recite some prayers while Leonid walked around the area of the mass grave, his face completely white. Before we left, I told everyone that I wanted to say the *kaddish*. Ilya protested that we had no minyan, but I felt that it was the appropriate thing to do. It was likely that nobody had ever said *kaddish* over the dead of Tolochin, and any *kaddish*, even one without a *minyan*, was better than no kaddish at all.

After what was a moving *kaddish* for all, we left the site. As we were leaving, we were approached by a woman who came out of a nearby house. She said that she recalled the screams of the dying Jews. Her mother and father told her that she had seen the Jews climbing on top of one another trying to escape the death pit, gasping for air. I won't write what my thoughts and feelings were.

A grave surrounded by a fence. At the center of the grave a young tree grows on top of the burial site

Near the entrance to the Jewish cemetery of Tolochin

From there, we traveled to the Jewish cemetery of Tolochin. Leonid visited the cemetery frequently and maintains the cemetery using personal funds. Once in the cemetery, Leonid went off by himself to repair some of the tombstones. I began to comb the cemetery for familiar names hoping to find the gravesite of a relative or an ancestor.

Most of the visible graves date from after the 1930s, and those are the ones which Leonid mostly tends. There is a whole section of the cemetery with tall grasses, broken tombstones which, over the decades, have turned into dense fields. I fought my way through the fields and did find some old graves. I also found many graves encircled by fences surrounded by trees and tall grasses.

There are literally a handful of graves which date prior to the revolution. After fighting my way through the deep shrubs, I encountered a well-preserved tombstone that belongs to Issak (Isser?) Moisivitch Merles, who was one of the wealthiest Jews of the town and whose home is now the current location of the museum of Tolochin. The Nazis tried to destroy his tombstone but weren't successful. There is a bullet hole in the top left-hand corner from a Nazi vandal.

However, one of the most notable moments for me was finding the gravesite of a distant cousin of mine named Nachum Rutstein. This is where my knowledge of the Cyrillic alphabet paid off and I was able to recognize my surname. I tried to clear some of the shrubs away which surrounded his grave but there was little I could do. I found a nearby tomb that was worn, and I could not read the name inscribed in it despite tracing the inscription with the black magic marker I brought.

The grave site of my cousin, Nachum Rutstein, in the Tolochin Jewish cemetery.

We couldn't spend more time in the cemetery, as we needed to get to the museum of Tolochin before it closed. So, with lots more to explore, we left and headed towards the center of town to visit the home of Issar

Moisivitch. As I was leaving, I noticed a grave that was separate from all the others. I thought that perhaps this individual had committed suicide or wasn't Jewish. Ilya said, possibly joking, that he was buried separately because he was a Polish Jew. Leonid said that he thought they had died during a difficult winter and they weren't able to bring his body to the center of the cemetery to be buried.

The separate grave mentioned.

After we left the cemetery, we dropped off Leonid at his home and drove to the center of town to visit the museum. The museum is located within what was once the home of one of the wealthiest Jews in town, Isser Merles. At the museum, we paid the entrance fee, and a guide took us around the entire museum explaining the exhibits. Tolochin was once seventy percent

Leonid Lifshitz leaving the Tolochin Jewish cemetery after locking the gates. Many of the grasses and fields in the background grow on top of old graves.

Jewish and founded by Jews, but there is not so much as a footnote in the museum about displaying what was once Jewish life. At the end of the tour, I told the guide who I was and why I had come to Tolochin. The guide quickly went into the other room and brought out the director of the museum. The director introduced herself as Irina Pikulik, and I told her why I came to Tolochin. I relayed to her the deep sense of curiosity, interest, and nostalgia that many Jews have towards Tolochin. I told her that I, too, was a child of Tolochin, and I wanted to know why there was no mention of the Jewish presence in the town. She told me that she wanted to have an exhibit about the Jewish presence in the town, but that she didn't have any information. Irina said that if she had information and material, she would surely put something together. Then, I took the kippah off my head and gave it to her, telling that it could be the first thing to exhibit about Jewish life. I told her that I would send her Judaica and I would try to get others to donate objects. She also began telling me a bit about the Jewish history of the town. Jews were said to have founded the town, which is named after a nearby river. At one point, Jews were over seventy percent and there were several waves of Jewish immigration to the West. She informed me that Issak Moisivitch Merles was a rich glassblower, founder of a factory and that the home museum is in his home[63]. Before I left, she gave me a gift - a thick book about Tolochin and some of its martyrs.

Once I left the museum, Dmitry and the others expressed their skepticism concerning the offer of the director to create an exhibit on the historical Jewish presence in Tolochin. The same sentiment was later expressed by other Jews in Minsk. However, I really do believe her, and I feel that her interest about the Jews and her commitment to creating an exhibit if given the material, were sincere. I have sent her some old Judaica with little expense to myself and I would encourage others to get in touch

The Museum of Tolochin and the former home of Isser Merles of Tolochin

---

[63] Irina Pikulik referred to him as "Issak Merles" while his tombstone read "Yisrael Merles." I think that I may have misheard or miswrote his name when speaking to the director. She likely meant to say, "Isser Merles."

with me about doing the same. The museum is located on Pionerskaya Street, #4 in Tolochin, Belarus.

Front: Mrs. Lifshitz, Luba Blechner, Tamara.
Back: Ilya, Yehuda, Dmitry in the Tolochin Park.

We then walked into the center of town, which is a few meters from the museum. As we were walking through the nearby park, we bumped into Mrs. Lifshitz, Tamara, and another Jew from Tolochin named Luba Blechner. We sat down at some nearby benches and spoke about the history of Jewish Tolochin, their current life challenges, and those that have left this little town. I realized that this little Jewish reunion could be one of its last, as it was likely that the Jewish presence in Tolochin would disappear within the next decade. It made me realize that the window to the past is closing quickly, and those who wish to make the journey need to make it now. There is little time left. We all said our goodbyes and exchanged contact information.

On our way back to Orsha, we drove through the town of Kochanova, where my great-great-grandfather, Dov Behr Rutstein, moved to from Tolochin. While Tolochin is a full-fledged town, Kochanova is a small village in the form of a single road with a dozen or two houses. When I asked if there were any Jews in Kochanova, I received different answers from different people.

I posit that my great-great-grandfather may have moved from Tolochin to Kochanova in his old age. It would have been cheaper to

The highway sign for Kochanova.

live in Kochanova than in Tolochin, and such an action may have been necessary after his entire family emigrated. Kochanova may have had a poorer population than of Tolochin and Orsha.

The road through Kochanova.

After leaving Tolochin, we drove back to Orsha and spent the night. Early the next morning, Dmitry and I returned to Minsk via the express train. I toured Minsk, and that evening, I met with a democracy activist that I had been corresponding with via the internet. She was brave, passionate, and dedicated to bringing about democratic changes to improve her country. She informed me of the recent election frauds and how the government had fooled the United Nations monitoring teams. She told me about how her university committed election fraud and how she and other students quietly protested. Unlike many other young, talented, and educated students her age, she has no plans to emigrate to the West but plans to stay and fight to improve Belarus. She wants Belarus to "join the rest of Europe." She told me she was embarrassed by her government's violations of human rights and its lack of freedom of speech. She wants the United States government to pressure her government to initiate democratic reforms. She also spoke about the mentality which is created by the lack of freedom. Too many people are content with the status quo and have no desire to become activists for freedom. For all the suffering, bitterness, and tragedy, which at

The Byelorussians KGB headquarters in Minsk, Belarus.

times seems to consume Belarus, she is a bright star in the night. My hope for a better future for Belarus resides in outstanding individuals like herself. My thoughts and prayers remain with her.

Thinking about her words, I began to understand a driving force behind Jewish emigration to the West in the last century. I believe that this may be one of the fundamental driving forces behind many migrations of the 20th century - freedom. Jews and non-Jews in Belarus are not free. If one does not live in a genuinely free society, one cannot maximize their existence. The words of Leonid rang through my head, "I worked really hard, nobody thanked me, and I got nothing in return — nothing." Dmitry said it even better when we were on the train, "people work really, really hard and they receive nothing in return…people are poor, and they are trying to figure out where their next meal will come from." People throughout Belarus work extremely hard and achieve nothing in return except for basic survival. It creates a culture of apathy and despair. Why do I have to work so hard if I will receive nothing in return?

I believe that one of the most important human needs is the feeling of personal satisfaction. Satisfaction comes from the things in our lives in which we take pride and define our own sense of what is best for us. Satisfaction often comes from an accomplishment, a situation, a project that we may have taken responsibility for, and which we achieved success. Other elements affect our deep and lasting satisfaction, such as the degree of effort we put into something. If I work really hard at university, I will have good grades. If I study for my LSAT's, I will do well on them. However, what happens when individuals put in tremendous effort and get nothing in return? What happens when an entire society does not see the fruits of its labors? What does an ambitious individual do in order to maximize their personal satisfaction and potential? Some stay in order to change their environment while most others decide to emigrate.

Putting these ideas together, I am restating a principle of Aristotle: satisfaction in life comes from exercising our abilities and thereby realizing our potential. The more complex and demanding the exercise of our realized capacities are, the greater the satisfaction. Opportunities to exercise our realized capacities depend on freedom. In a communist or totalitarian state, our ability to maximize our satisfaction and potential is stifled. We cannot take responsibility for our destinies because our destinies are not our own but that of our rulers. Without controlling our destinies, we cannot truly reach our potential as human beings. Places such as the United States allow us to reach our potential as human beings if we choose. This is what I believe was a factor in the emigration of millions to the shores of the United States. In the words of Irving Berlin, also a son of Tolochin, "God bless America from sea to shining sea."

The next morning, I woke up before dawn. Waiting for Leonid to drive me to the airport, I read a description of my great-grandfather Yaakov Rutstein written by my grandfather Milton Rothstein. Milton wrote:

> *"In the beginning, my father was a great "maven," a genius who far exceeded his father's business prowess. At the age of six, he was taken to the market (farmers and commodities) and he dealt with the Russian peasant buying various things, horsehair (bristles), produce, furs and pelts. At the end of the day, he earned more than my grandfather who was a giant of a man called "Dov Behr" in Hebrew or Yiddish? He was over 6'4 weighing 270 pounds with powerful muscles. He was a "gibbur" and was reputed to have killed many Cossacks who had massacred poor defenseless Jews in pogroms. Yankov went to heder until the age of twelve. During his school days, he engaged in many activities such as waldsacher {lumber merchant in Yiddish}. He could estimate the output of an orchard for trade and anticipated accompanying his father to market. He was hired by a German company to export seafood from Russia as General Manager. He accumulated quite a fortune, which later was deposited in London, where he ran away from the Russian army during the Russo-Sino (Japanese) war. He was stricken with rheumatic fever in route to the U.S.*

175

After months of hospitalization and using up all his money, he landed in N.Y. practically penniless..."

My thoughts turned to my great-grandparents. After experiencing Tolochin, a place that has barely changed, my imagination took me back to the small shtetl of yore. I realized that exactly a hundred years earlier, in the summer of 1905, my great-grandfather, Yaakov Rutstein, left his small village in search of a better life. There must have been a certain naiveté to him, a young country boy leaving for America to maximize his potential. I can imagine him packing some dense whole wheat loaves and heading towards the train station with only a small backpack. I could imagine the journey to Libau, Poland. Maybe, he spent a day or two in each city he passed through. Maybe, he stayed with distant cousins in each. Getting on the boat to America, even the non-superstitious or non-religious Jew would have said a prayer before leaving for America. I am sure that Yaakov was no exception.

Dov Behr and Riva Shpitzgluz Rutstein of Tolochin, Belarus. These are my great-great grandparents. Photo: Tolochin, Belarus; circa 1910.

Jimmy Kaplan, a descendant of Jacob Rutstein, once wrote, "I was talking with my wife last night, after reading her some selections from Milton's story, and we contemplated what it must have been like to come over here from Russia under the conditions that are so foreign to us. It must have taken enormous determination and vision to want to travel so far to start a new life. This past year, we were able to see a touring production of Fiddler on the Roof, which starred Theodore Bikel. Despite his age (over 80!), he is still full of enormous energy and power...When I think of all the villagers leaving at the end, it's not hard to imagine a young Jacob being one of them, whose family sent him to America with their highest hopes.

ADDENDUM

History of Jewish Life

The Assistant Director of the Religious Communities of Belarus describes life in the Orsha-Tolochin region prior to the revolution:

> *Orsha was founded in 1067, and the first Jewish presence in the city is recorded in the sixteenth century. Historically, Orsha was a very small town but by the turn of the century, that began to change, and the city grew drastically. It was the largest city in the region and a railroad center. By the mid 19ʰ century, there was a revolution in manufacturing, especially in the lumber industry, which originated in Siberia. In 1890, there was electricity in Orsha, and today it has evolved into a city of nearly 110, 000 people.*

> *Yiddish was once one of the four official languages of Belarus. Most people, including Jews, were illiterate, but when boys were five years old, they were taught some of the basics of the Torah in cheder. Religion was taught in the home first, and then children picked up the rest in a cheder and then, in some cases, went on to Yeshiva. Girls were taught at home, and there were special professional schools for girls. No girls went to Yeshiva. There was a Lubavitch presence in Orsha as the Lubavitch city of Lyady was nearby. Historically, Belarus was part of the Kingdom of Lithuania, and thus, most of the population adhered to the Lithuanian tradition. However, there was a small Lubavitch presence. The Orsha and Tolochin regions were stuck in the middle of two great spheres of influence, that of the Litvaks and Chasidic, yet most were*

Litvaks, but there were some poor Jews that were attracted to Chasidim[64].

The pogroms triggered the massive wave of Jewish emigration to the West, but poverty also played a lesser role. Jews went to America illegally. Jews said everything and did everything they could do buy tickets. They formed special committees and hired Russians to help them escape Russia. There were two ways to leave Belarus. Jews went both legally and illegally. In the latter case, there were natural barriers to pass, and the government would actively hunt those who tried to escape, and many died trying to leave Russia. Sometimes the government actively encouraged Jews to leave. All a Jew needed was money. Many Jews would sell everything they own, and only then would they have enough money to file an application for a passport to leave the country.

During the First World War, the Germans were very polite to the Jews. During World War Two, many Jews expected the same thing. Most Byelorussians were indifferent to the Nazi persecution of the Jews, and many actively assisted them. In Dubrovna, where his family is from, the town population actively assisted the Nazis in removing the Jewish population. Dubrovna was a small shtetl just like Tolochin.

In Soviet times, there were quotas against Jews in higher education. Stalin died on Purim which many Byelorussian Jews felt was symbolic.

---

[64] I met a man in Orsha who was anti-Chabad. He didn't know the Aleph-Bet, but he knew that he was a Litvak. He was proud and resented the Chabad encroachment in what was historically Litvak territory.

A lot of people complained about the Chabad presence in Orsha. The most common complaint was the Rabbi lives in a luxurious apartment and doesn't share his wealth with the people and wont provides service to members who are not part of his community.

Various Photographs

Random Jewish grave site in the Orsha Cemetery.

A photograph of a man who may have been Adolph "Eydola" Lipshitz of Tolochin and the grandfather of Leonid Lipshitz.

A home being built on the outskirts of Tolochin.

*A memorial for the Jews of Tolochin at the site of the mass grave near the
village of Raitsy.*

Bertha (Breina) Poretzkyn (1900-1983)

Bertha was the youngest sister of Basha Poretzky (daughter of Tzvi Hirsch), my great-grandmother. According to Professor Zvi Gitelman, Bertha is dressed in a Russian peasant dress and is playing a native guitar. This photo, circa 1915, illustrates the extent of her russification in contrast to some of her other siblings. All of the eight Poretsky children reacted to the tumultuous ideological climate in different ways. Some became Zionists, Socialists, and Capitalists, while others remained traditionalists.

Zalman Kalatin - The Last "Rabbi" of Tolochin

According to Ilya Halfey, Zalman Kalatin was the last spiritual leader of Tolochin. In 1960, Zalman had a "golden" fiftieth wedding anniversary in Tolochin. Ilya remembers people who are playing the violin and dancing. Everything was kosher about the wedding, including the food and chuppah. Ilya remembers people praying, wearing tefillin and tallaisim. When Judaism was not permitted during the Soviet era, the Jews prayed secretly in the rabbi's house even though it was illegal. There was no room in the house because so many people wanted to pray, so they put the children outside. Ilya remembers trying to untie the knots on the tallaism as a child. Jews worked in the market and in making clothing. Lots of Jews worked in the lumber industry.

The Last "Rabbi" of Tolochin, Zalman Kalatin.

182

Mrs. (Tamara?) Lifshitz

Mrs. Lifshitz was born in the village of Uchala\Ucvalah, which is in the Minsk region. In 1941, the Germans took over her village. They gathered all the Jews into five houses where eighty Jews were killed on the first day. For one year, the Jewish inhabitants of the town were together in five houses. On March 1, 1942, the Nazis issued an order to shoot the Jewish people living in these homes. Only ten people escaped the shootings, and she was one of them.

She eventually found herself walking alone in the forest (for three months?) with another girl named Bella (Kroyck). She

Mrs. Lipshitz with her medals.

remembers being hungry and eating grass in order to survive. She was crying throughout telling her story, and Dmitry, my translator, was having trouble understanding some of the details. On July 8th, the partisans found them. They took her, and she joined the resistance. In the resistance, she worked in the kitchen. She would defend the kitchen with her gun. She was only eleven years old.

Sometimes she would take her gun and shoot things and eat them, and sometimes she didn't eat at all. Sometimes they would attack the Germans and kill them, and she would retrieve their guns and food. She was doing all this at the age of eleven. She spent nearly four years with the partisans. At the end of the war, she found herself in a village near Tolochin called Slavc. It was there that the partisans connected with the soviet army. She was not drafted into the army because she was so young but instead was sent to an orphanage. At 16, she started working at a cement factory and excelled at her work. She received many medals. Mrs. Lipshitz was so proud of her medals that she ran to her room to show me them. She eventually came to settle in Tolochin because she had an aunt who lived there.

Tamara Abramovna Kahovich

Before the war, most of Tolochin was farmland. Her father was the director of the farms owned by Abraham Kravashay, who owned three farms. Most of the houses that exist now were farmland before the war. There was a local farm named "Karkali," which was a Jewish name. So, during the Soviet era, they changed it to Victory farm, but it hasn't changed back since. It was easier and cheaper to live on the outskirts of town. When they lived in Tolochin, it was harder and more expensive. Her (grand?)mother's surname was Furmann and her father was Mendel, who worked in "metalwork." Her grandmother, Basya Furhman, was involved in local conflict resolution. Because of her grandmother's local stature, her mother was taken in by a Russian family and saved. Her mother had watched the Nazis kill her brother and grandmother. The neighbors' agreed to hide her mother in their house. The Russians came eventually, and they evacuated. The family only came back after 1946. Tamara was born in 1944.

Basya and Bracha Furhman of Tolochin, Belarus.

Tamara was somehow related to the Lipshitz family. I believe this is how: There where two Furhman sisters. One was Basyia, and the other was Bracha. Basiya's granddaughter was Tamara. Bracha Furhman married into the Lipshitz family and was the mother of Leonid.

Luba Blechner Blackman

I met Luba randomly in the center of Tolochin. Her father was Benyamin and was a roof maker. She had a brother that went to the USA before the war. She was six when the war started and was evacuated to Tashkent.

Misha Ginsberg

Misha was born in 1946 in Belarus. His father drove a carriage for a living and his mother was a housewife. His father also worked as a shoemaker and was illiterate. Misha has three older sisters one of which is in Germany. Misha went to school at the age of eight, which is considered late, because his family had no money. During World War II, his father went off to the war while his mother went to Ural with the children. Because his father was illiterate, he could not send letters to his family because he couldn't write or read and as a result the family never knew if he was safe. After the war, Misha's father worked as a chimney cleaner. His mother was from Mogilev, but his fathers' family has lived in Orsha for many generations. His mother, from the Ganetska family, was from a rich family which moved to Orsha from Mogiliew.

Misha had an uncle that married Russian women and had five children. The uncle went to the Russian, and the kids went to another village to hide. Someone ratted them to the authorities and subsequently, the children were taken and killed. After the war, some wanted revenge for the killings and subsequently, killed the tattler.

About the Author

Yehuda "J.R." Rothstein is a real estate and construction counsel at an in-house tech company. Previously, he was a Fulbright visiting scholar at the University of Toronto Faculty of Law, where he focused on Comparative Real Estate transactions.

Mr. Rothstein is also a transactional attorney who practices on an extensive range of matters in both practice groups with both law firm and in-house counsel experience. His real estate law practice includes development, acquisitions and dispositions, and leasing transactions of real property. During his career, Mr. Rothstein has worked with numerous corporate and individual clients, including property managers, investors, developers, and cooperatives. He provides legal support and advice on all real estate matters. His legal advice goes beyond the law and responds creatively and strategically to meet business needs. Mr. Rothstein, who studies part-time real estate development at New York University, is a real estate investor himself and often assists his clients in syndicating real estate deals.

Mr. Rothstein received his Juris Doctor from Cornell Law School, where he was Editor of the Journal of Law and Public Policy and an Albert Heit Scholarship recipient. He simultaneously obtained an L.LM. Master of Laws in International and Comparative Law from Cornell Law. After receiving his J.D. and L.LM., Mr. Rothstein began his legal career serving as a federal law clerk in the Eastern District of New York for the Honorable I. Leo Glasser. He later worked at a Midtown Manhattan law firm practicing real estate law.

Mr. Rothstein completed his undergraduate studies at the University of Michigan. After university, he was a Legacy

Heritage Fellow doing human rights at the United Nations. Later, Mr. Rothstein was an Ariana De Rothschild Fellow at the University of Cambridge Judge Business School in Cambridge, United Kingdom, focusing on Social Entrepreneurship and impact investing with faith-based communities.

Today, Mr. Rothstein is a member of DOROT, Sons of the American Revolution, and the NAACP. He also serves as a member of the Steering and Board of AJC ACCESS. Mr. Rothstein has lived, worked, studied, and traveled to over two dozen countries. He grew up in Monsey, New York.